WE'RE NOT COLORBLIND

HEALING THE RACIAL DIVIDE

Dr. Alveda King
&
Ginger Howard

Scripture quotations marked KJV are from the King James Version of the Bible.

Scripture quotations marked NIV are taken from the Holy Bible, New International Version®, NIV®. Copyright © 1973, 1978, 1984, 2011 by Biblica, Inc.™ Used by permission of Zondervan. All rights reserved worldwide. www.zondervan.com. The "NIV" and "New International Version" are trademarks registered in the United States Patent and Trademark Office by Biblica, Inc.™

Scripture quotations marked NKJV are taken from the New King James Version®. Copyright © 1982 by Thomas Nelson. Used by permission. All rights reserved.

Scripture quotations marked NLT are from the Holy Bible, New Living Translation, copyright © 1996, 2004, 2007. Used by permission of Tyndale House Publishers, Inc., Wheaton, IL 60189. All rights reserved.

Scripture quotations marked The Message are from The Message: The Bible in Contemporary English, copyright © 1993, 1994, 1995, 1996, 2000, 2001, 2002. Used by permission of NavPress Publishing Group.

For world wide distribution

ISBN: 9781087910246

ISBN: 9781663554260 (Barnes & Noble)

ISBN: 9798676953829 (KDP)

LCCN: 2020916092

Stanton Publishing House
Howard Publishing House
PO Box 550695
Atlanta, GA 30355
www.werenotcolorblindbook.com
contact@werenotcolorblindbook.com

ENDORSEMENTS

"At a time in our nation, when racial division seems to be escalating, Dr. Alveda King and Ginger Howard speak truth to the divide-we are one blood and one race. They remind us to celebrate our differences through the lens of God's love. If you want to be a part of the solution, I highly recommend that you read this book."

MIKE LINDELL,
CEO MY PILLOW, INC.

"In *We're Not Colorblind*, Alveda and Ginger invite the reader to engage in a conversation about race from a biblical worldview. In offering a fresh and positive perspective that is grounded in faith, this book is instrumental in bridging the racial divide in our polarized nation."

RALPH REED,
FOUNDER AND CHAIRMAN OF
FAITH AND FREEDOM COALITION

"I have known Dr. Alveda King and Ms. Ginger Howard for more than two decades. I am so grateful that they were led to write this very important book; a must-read. If God can use any two people to be His instruments of love, peace, and forgiveness, it would be these two amazingly loving ambassadors of the Prince of peace. Hate may be grabbing the headline news, but let's make this message of love overwhelm evil."

MICHAEL YOUSSEF, PHD.

"*We're Not Colorblind – Healing the Racial Divide* is an OPEN door into the hearts and minds of TWO Very Special Women of God: One Black: Dr. Alveda C. King and One White: Ginger Howard, yet, arguably, as you will read, ONE and the same; In heart, in purpose, in passion and in LIFE… in bringing UNITY to ALL who seek to divide, steal, kill and destroy— and HOW, through commonality and Christ, THEY are doing just that! A moving and hopeful read that breathes HEALING instead of HURT, and HOPE instead of PAIN… and powerfully so! "Blessed are the peacemakers, for they shall be called the children of God." (Matthew 5:19)

JENSINE BARD, FOUNDER AND CEO,
JENSINE BARD MINISTRIES, INC.

"In *We're Not Colorblind,* Alveda and Ginger model authentic friendship despite quite different racial origins and life experiences. Using God's Word as their solid foundation, they provide urgently needed keys to healing the racial divide, helping all Americans move from hate to love, from bitterness to forgiveness, and from suspicion to trust. This timely book is a must-read at an urgent time in our national journey, helping us to realize that we all share "one blood" and that unconditional love is possible through our Heavenly Father."

BOB DEES
MAJOR GENERAL, U.S. ARMY,
RETIRED PRESIDENT,
NATIONAL CENTER FOR HEALTHY VETERANS

"Finally, a book on racism that will both open your mind and soften your heart, if you let it."

DAVID DEUEL PHD,
SENIOR RESEARCH FELLOW AND POLICY ADVISOR
THE CHRISTIAN INSTITUTE ON DISABILITY AT JONI AND FRIENDS

"If you are interested in unmasking the fears that hinder your desire to bridge the gaps in the world around you through deep conversations and Christlike love, this book is a valuable inspiration. The devil has a way of using our past to manipulate us and hold back our progress, but Dr. Alveda King and Ginger Howard have victoriously cast this aside to pursue a great cause and inspire others along the way."

EMMANUEL-LA TARR
LIBERIAN STUDENT, LIBERTY UNIVERSITY

"Alveda King is the most loving prophetic voice in America on issues of justice, life and healing our racism. She can always open our eyes with loving truth."

ALLAN PARKER PRESIDENT,
THE JUSTICE FOUNDATION

"My sisters, Alveda and Ginger have provided readers with a guide to understanding God's Mosaic of Humankind and the Kingdom-focused unity necessary to honor it."

AMBASSADOR KEN BLACKWELL
DISTINGUISHED FELLOW
FAMILY RESEARCH COUNCIL

"Dr. Alveda C. King and Ginger Howard's book caused me to reflect on how much our world is in need of racial reconciliation. *We're Not Colorblind* is a must-read for those who desire to be reconciled to one another. I would personally recommend that churches and faith based organizations study this book as a teaching tool."

OLIVER RICHMOND
PRESIDENT, THE KINGDOM PARTNERS

"*We're Not Colorblind* comes at a pivotal moment in a time of unrest in America. This message brings eternal love, forgiveness, and reconciliation and is more than a book. It's matters of the heart that will bring inner healing to your soul to be loved, and love people, without glasses. Dr. Alveda King and Ginger's transparency in this book is the beginning of a conversation to bring healing and reconciliation in our nation. I'm inspired by reading this book to love people so radically they wonder why!!!"

HENRY BECERRA SENIOR PASTOR,
CITY CHURCH INTERNATIONAL

"Alveda King is uniquely positioned to help heal the land and the racial divide that has caused too much pain for too long. With fresh eyes on an old problem and a keen understanding of the history of racism in and beyond America, this book will give you hope and strategies to defeat racism."

JENNIFER LECLAIRE FOUNDER,
AWAKENING HOUSE OF PRAYER

"The legacy of Dr. MLK lives on in his niece Dr. Alveda King. Through her profound life experiences, God has shown her true roots of the demonic evil that divides people according to ethnicity. Her journey with Ginger is an example for all of us in this period of civil unrest. I highly endorse this compelling book."

DR. JOSEPH MATTERA

"With insights into Alveda's response to the assassination of her uncle Dr. Martin Luther King, her faith journey which has taken her to be a spokesperson sent from Jesus to our hurting nation; the blending of Ginger's strong yet healing words complement each other so wonderfully. The content of this message is something all Americans should read."

STEVE REITER, CEO

DXM360 ADVISORY AND INTEGRATION SERVICES

"Dr. Martin Luther King, Jr. certainly could never have foreseen that more than a half century after his assassination, his beloved niece, Dr. Alveda King would be decades-long into taking up his cause, and the Lord's cause, for racial reconciliation and beyond that, racial understanding. This book is as much a life story as it is a further revelation from God on the cause of racial, economic and social justice.

This is a story that simply MUST be told. My friend for years now, who allows me to call her Alveda, has teamed up with her dear friend who is "fair, not white," as she puts it, Ginger Howard. Together, this is their compelling story of how they remain "not colorblind," nor should they be such, because it was God who made such beautiful hues of skin colors and, who are we to deny ourselves or anyone of His enjoyment of the same. *We're Not Colorblind* is certainly a fresh revelation that most, among all the ethnic groups, have yet to consider. Grab a cup of coffee and let's read it again, together! Please, get this book and, while you're at it, why not pick up another copy for your friends!

STEVE SHULTZ, FOUNDER,
THE ELIJAH LIST

"This is a timely book addressing what we need to hear the most; true unity in our values and purpose contrasting the increasing racial divide. As business owners, ministers, speakers and authors ourselves, we value the content this book conveys. As always, Dr. Alveda King brings a softer, balanced approach to the hardline anger found in our nation today. We applaud Dr. King and Ginger Howard on sharing their experiences and vision in a loving manner."

MIKE, TRISHA AND ARIANNA FOX
SPLASH DESIGNWORKS, LLC.

"The racial healing that our nation longs for will be accomplished when people follow the 'Alveda-Ginger model' of meaningful and constructive personal dialogue. And there is a 'third person' who needs to be in that process. It is amazing what can happen between two people of different ethnicities when they invite the Holy Spirit into the conversation."

DR. JIM GARLOW, CEO,
WELL VERSED

"From different walks of life, Alveda and Ginger came together to write a book on racial issues. Alveda from the rich history of the Martin Luther King family, and Ginger from white America, share how their hearts knit together to tell their story of love beyond color."

CAROL EVERETT,
FOUNDER, THE HEIDI GROUP

Racism is nothing new. Even the Apostle Peter struggled with his own racial bias, confessed his sin, and crossed the racial divide in his time. As a result, he, having come from a marginalized community, and Cornelius, having come from a privileged position and serving as a law enforcement officer, had an important transformational conversation that provided a template for us. (See Acts 10:28-35) *We're Not Colorblind* is a refreshing, hopeful, and inspirational book that provides us with very practical ways to build upon our experience in fracturing our present cultural barriers.

Dr. Alveda King and Ginger Howard have presented a pragmatic work that calls those motivated in faith to step forward and build bridges that will withstand the stress which happens when cultures intertwine. Consider this book a first step to the relationship building efforts that we so desperately need as a people of God, and as a nation.

PASTOR MIKE BERRY
ANNAPOLIS, MARYLAND

"The Lord is always right on time. *We're Not Colorblind* is the salve needed for our national wounds. Both old and new. Alveda and Ginger do the reader an immediate service by drawing the reader's attention to their own frailties in contrast to God's never-ending reparation of the human heart through the cross of His Son, Jesus Christ. The transparency with which both of these sisters of the same spiritual family share, is a refreshing reminder that God's first purpose is always people and His first priority is our freedom. Co-laborers in Christ, these accomplished, dynamic women of God have opened the door to generational healing that only love through honesty and humility can offer. Praise the Lord."

MONICA MATTHEWS
NATIONAL MEDIA PERSONALITY,
CLEAR TALK MEDIA

This is only a partial list of endorsements; full list available at https://www.werenotcolorblindbook.com/

ACKNOWLEDGMENTS

From Ginger...

There are so many people that helped birth this book. I first want to thank my Heavenly Father, who gave me a dream to write this book. Secondly, I want to thank my precious friend and sister in Christ, Alveda King, who immediately said yes when I shared my dream with her. And to my darling and brilliant spiritual daughter and friend, Emily Woods, without whom this book would not have been possible. She spent countless hours poring over my thoughts and words and editing and re-editing until the final product was ready to print.

I also want to thank my prayer partners who prayed this book into being. I am most grateful and indebted to these strong prayer warriors who prayed through this project with me. These amazing women of God stood in the gap with me, Ann Platz Groton, Amy Heifner, Carol Taylor, Jamie Ayers, Martha Kimbel, Taffy Dunlevie, Elise Wilkes, Lee Anne Cowart, Marsha Conrad, Carol Swayze, Anne Catherman, Elizabeth Weatherby, Connie Musselman, and Andrea Denton. And to the late Ann Kieffer, who went on to glory before the finished product, and whose prayers have lived on. My mother, Beth McClelland, prayed constantly about this book, and her prayers always are such a blessing and encouragement to me.

Last, but not least, this book would not have been published if Dr. Clarice Fluitt had not spoken into my life and had the confidence in me to share her amazing team with me. Thank you, Dr. Clarice, Dr. Tandie Mazule, Dr. Evon Peet, and Carol Martinez. Thanks also to Kevin Keller, who designed our cover. All of you are co-laborers in this endeavor, and to God be all the glory!

DEDICATION

To Robert and Will,

You give me hope for our future generations. May your kind and loving hearts help lead others to not be colorblind and to see all through the eyes of God.

With all my love,

Aunt Ginger

Dr. Alveda and Her Grandfather
Art by: Tony Smith

ACKNOWLEDGMENTS

From Alveda...

This book is a journal of a journey of love. Each and everyone I've ever met, and some I have not met yet admired from a distance, are part of this experience. There are too many to reference here, and I don't want to run the risk of leaving anyone out. Therefore, I acknowledge and dedicate this book to God with thanksgiving for everyone and everything that has been a part of this life experience along the way.

Thanks, Ginger, for taking this book journey with me.

Lovingly,

Evangelist Alveda C. King

———————◉———————

"I thank my GOD upon every remembrance
of [each and every one of] you."

— Philippians 1:3 —

———————◉———————

TABLE OF CONTENTS

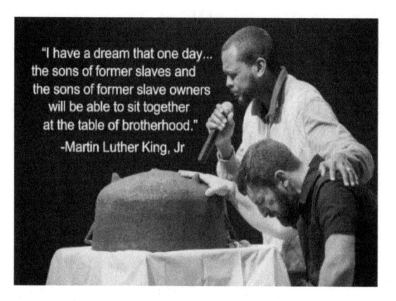

Pictured: Will Ford with Matt Lockett

FOREWORD

Harry R. Jackson Jr.

I have known Dr. Alveda King for over 15 years. She and Ginger Howard have written a book that will help people overcome the foundational issues that have fueled the fear and the racism of our day. I met Ginger Howard on a trip to Tulsa, Oklahoma, on which we attended a Christian reconciliation event and a political rally. I was impressed by their personal relationship and their personal commitment to political and social change.

In this forward, I will simply address three things:

1. Why is this book needed at this time?

2. Who are these authors, and what are their credentials to speak to these issues?

3. What are the truths that the culture must rethink if we are going to heal the racial divide?

Why is this book needed at this time?

In the Bible, David discovers that the giant Goliath has been taunting the army of Israel. David asks one rhetorical question before he dives into the conflict. He asks those around him, "Is there not a cause?" Better stated, "Is there a reason to enter a national battle?"

The deaths of George Floyd, Breonna Taylor, and Ahmaud Arbery have launched fresh international interest in the civil rights movement. The national riots and impending ongoing, urban violence have brought us to a point that the nation is ready for national police reform and healing of the racial divide. There is a cause for us to advance towards these goals.

These authors believe that America's ethnic tensions and injustices can be healed on our watch. It is obvious that the younger generation of minorities has grown weary in well-doing. Their outrage and demands have been a shot heard around the world.

There have been demonstrations on three continents. The Black Lives Matter organization has been ramping up for nearly six or seven years since 2013 and the death of Michael Brown in Ferguson, Missouri, in 2014. There has also been a cry from the entire next generation's minority community for equity and equal access to the American Dream.

During the same time, anger and division have been brewing, many Christian groups have been praying for a day when members of the church once again lead the way. Some have written somewhat of a divine prescription to this nation's original sins; racism and greed.

In the wake of this wave, five years ago, Alveda King, Bernice King, Andrew Young and nearly 200 other Christian leaders of various major denominations and social action groups, representing 40 million believers, gathered at the Potter's House in Dallas, Texas, for a high-level series of round table meetings and an evening gathering attracting over 7,000 attendees. We gathered for communion and prayer that evening. The date was Thursday, January 15, 2015, which happened to be Dr. Martin Luther King's actual birthday that year, rather than the national holiday.

During that time, "The Reconciled Church Movement" attempted to give guidelines for the Church to lead the way in healing the racial divide in our nation, invoking the Church's common outlook, practice, and coordinated action. We developed a strategic approach that we called "Bridges To Peace." These "Bridges" were seven initiatives we could engage that could help unite the entire Christian church.

As a Christian Evangelist and popular leader of the pro-life movement, behind the scenes, Dr. Alveda King also champions criminal justice reform, opportunity zones, positive media and entertainment, and minority home-ownership initiatives. I believe that Dr. Alveda King has had a strong prophetic sense that violence would be at the doors if something significant was not done to change the trajectory.

Over two years ago, Alveda and Ginger began to write and develop an amazing theological concept which emphasizes that all human life is sacred and that we are all of "one blood" and "one human race." Using Acts 17:26-27 as their base, they build their case.

The verses read as follows:

"As from one man He made all nations, that they should inhabit the whole earth; and He marked out their appointed times in history and the boundaries of their lands. God did this so they would seek Him and perhaps reach out for Him, though He is not far from any of us." (NIV)

If we are one blood, we cannot claim superiority or inferiority. Truly one blood means that we are actually one human race. One equal human race who, if given the same opportunities, can achieve the same goals.

As fate would have it, the violence we feared years ago is now at our door. Thankfully, Alveda King and Ginger Howard have prepared a practical directive for all Americans.

A unique aspect of this book is that it is written by two ethnically different women. Women are the first teachers in the home, they are the purveyors of culture, and they teach a biblical worldview or pass on prejudice. Yet, this book is not just to be read by women; it's for every individual, family, church, and community.

What are the qualifications of the authors to speak on healing America?

Both of the authors are immensely qualified to offer solutions and strategies to heal the racial divide in our nation. Both are Christian women with a biblical worldview. Above all, their mutual respect and love inform their strategies.

Further, they are both savvy women grounded in both politics and business. Ginger Howard is a national committeewoman for the Republican National Committee. She understands the process and strategic role of politics in our national transformation. She is also an accomplished businesswoman who has succeeded in the fast-paced fashion industry after graduating from the University of Georgia. In 2014, Ginger also founded ATH Consulting, Inc., a political consulting firm. The firm seeks to support Christian candidates. This is important because structural changes in our culture will require public policy changes along with business and faith organizations working together.

Finally, with Ginger's background and effervescent personality, she and Alveda have become covenant sisters. Together they demonstrate that we all can heal a dimension of the racial divide on a personal level.

The personal commitment to social change keeps us from being hypocritical. Our next step can be a significant step because we can lead the way forward towards national change.

As far as Dr. Alveda is concerned, her active engagement as a youth organizer in the 20th Century Civil Rights Movement is part of the "King Family Legacy" where her family's Christian roots and civil rights credentials are to be acknowledged by anyone who works in the civil rights arena. Alveda applies this experience to her contributions toward the protection of the sanctity of life here in the 21st Century.

Further, most people are unaware that Alveda has served as a Georgia State Representative, a presidential appointee and has an earned MBA. She is accomplished in media, entertainment, and the arts. She is also a devoted mother and grandmother.

In addition, she and others in her family have mastered Dr. Martin Luther King, Jr.'s strategies in non-violent protests and social change.

What are the truths that the culture must rethink if we are going to heal the racial divide?

The authors' insights are listed and clearly prioritized in the table of contents. Fortunately, the very first chapter articulates that racism must be dealt with as a heart issue, first of all.

For 400 years, since the first slaves arrived on our American shores, the church has sided with the secular community instead of prophetically calling the nation to repentance.

In the pre-civil war era, only a remnant of Christians called abolitionists was brave enough to stand up for the truth. During the civil rights movement, many Caucasians shed their blood with Blacks, called Negroes at the time, to create an atmosphere of justice for all humankind.

Nonetheless, Christian reformers succeeded in bringing the nation and the Western World this far. Thankfully, we are not finished yet.

Howard and King have not written a book on race to blame and to shame. They have written a road map to national unity.

The Christian call for the body of Christ to love one another is the place that Ginger Howard and Alveda King begin their journey. We must meet them there.

Laws and structural reformation can only govern the external behavior of humanity. The American Dream requires internal insight through the Word of God and self-discipline ignited by the Holy Spirit of God. If you are Caucasian (White) today, you are not the problem. If you are White in this generation, you didn't create racism. If you are White, as Americans, you do have a glorious opportunity to help create a new America; a greater America than ever before.

If you are Black, Hispanic, or Asian/Pacific Islander, native-born, or transported to our shores as Black, Brown, Red, and Yellow Americans; regardless of our ethnicities, we can all step forward and address America's future by living out her creeds and beliefs daily.

As the title of the book declares, 'We Can Heal the Racial Divide.' We can do this on our watch!

Therefore, read, reflect, and act!

This is a must-read, written by two women who have lived its truth.

INTRODUCTION

Emily Woods

To say that we need a new perspective on politics in our country is an understatement. The divisive, jaded, and dark culture that surrounds the political realm is destructive and disheartening. In spite of this, I believe there are riches of untapped potential in politics—in policy-making and in politician-ing—that we have yet to dig into!

Picture this: Politics becomes synonymous with problem-solving. Politicians are humble and inquisitive, hungering to learn the concerns of their constituents because they sincerely care about the well-being of the people they represent. Democrats and Republicans see themselves as allies, not as enemies, and they deeply value each other's voices. Conservative and liberal thought processes are viewed as complementary, as a needed balance that creates productive tension. (I picture a situation similar to King Arthur and the Knights of the Round Table, where leaders see themselves as being on the same team for the good of their nation, and they gather around to develop a strategic battle plan to protect and prosper their entire land.) As far as the media, though natural leanings are to be expected, imagine news stations enabling us to simply learn about different perspectives on current events and not inundate us with trash-talking and blindly biased coverage. At the end of the day, we as voters see our leaders as people who will make decisions to not just benefit us personally, but as policy-makers that we hold accountable to also better the lives of as many other people as possible.

Is something like this even possible? I believe it is. But in order for politics to change, we the people have work to do. We must advocate for laws and leaders that align with values of empathy and justice, but we must hold ourselves accountable to empathize and act justly in our daily lives. We have to first come to terms with our own stories and the messiness we feel: being broken and yet hopeful, fearful and yet loving, tired and yet passionate, ashamed and yet forgiven. And then we have to believe, in our heart of hearts, that every person has a story worth listening to and learning from—and then take initiative to create the spaces to listen and learn from each other.

Though movements and marches are rallying behind the cause of social justice, racial reconciliation has yet to set in. Large gatherings are important because they raise awareness and create a sense of unity, but they don't seem to be healing wounds or changing hearts. I believe true healing and deeper unity will come when we don't just gather in the streets, but when we gather around tables, breaking bread and sharing stories in the intimacy of friendship. When we create space around tables for honesty, for new perspectives, and for deeper understanding, our hearts and minds will be changed toward "the other" who has become our new brother or sister.

More than anything, we have to approach each other with humility and mercy. The answers to the societal problems we face are anything but simple, and our personal stories and national history are layered with complexity. Peeling back those layers to discover the roots of our pain will be vulnerable and uncomfortable, but without conversations to air out the wounds from the past, the dark depths of bitterness and fear will remain. But I believe that if we the people have the courage to have hard conversations amongst ourselves, we can empower conversations being had by our leaders. By gathering around our own dinner tables and opening our hearts and minds to each other, we the people can change the conversations happening around tables that shape business, healthcare, education, housing, and transportation. When we the people are able to lower our fists and put politics aside, we will find ourselves with new vision, new friends, and new leaders guiding our nation to true reconciliation.

In the months ahead, I am praying for a fresh harvest of friendships to be cultivated across our land. I pray that the Lord softens the soil of our hearts, tills the ground with grace, and plants a love for our neighbor that takes root in the depths of America's soul. I pray that we see a flourishing of friendships that go beyond the boundaries of political parties, ethnic groups, cultures, and beliefs. And as friendships grow, may we find freedom from the darkness that threatens to divide and destroy us. I pray that we are not paralyzed by the pain of the past nor the drama of politics; but instead, may we be driven forward by a furious love for our neighbor, clinging to the hope of what we can do to heal and reconcile with each other.

It is up to us, the people of America, to write the rest of our story. May we command our hearts to take courage in the midst of the battle that awaits us; may we love each other and our God more fiercely than ever before. May we treasure our freedom, and may we cherish the blood that was shed to secure it. For "greater love has no one than this: to lay down one's life for one's friends" (John 15:13). Here's to fighting for greater love in the months ahead, my friends. The future of our country depends on it.

Chapter One

A MEETING OF THE HEARTS

———◈———

*From one blood God made all people, [so] that they should
inhabit the whole earth; and God marked out their appointed
times in history and the boundaries of their lands. God did this
so that they would seek God and perhaps reach out for God and
find God, though God is not far from any one of us. 'For in God
we live and move and have our being.' As some of your own
poets have said, 'We are God's offspring.'*

—Acts 17: 26-28 (NIV)—

———◈———

*"WE MUST LEARN TO LIVE TOGETHER AS
BROTHERS OR PERISH TOGETHER AS FOOLS."*

—Reverend Dr. Martin Luther King Jr.—

Alveda Speaks

My uncle, the Reverend Dr. Martin Luther King Jr. (hereafter referred to as Uncle ML) was assassinated on April 4, 1968, in Memphis, Tennessee. While much had been accomplished in the fight for racial equality, his death catapulted the whole world into a state of flux and confusion. Violence was now erupting in corridors that heretofore had coexisted—sometimes peacefully, sometimes uncomfortably.

In the fall of 1968, just months after my uncle had been assassinated, I was a freshman at Murray State University in Kentucky. I had two roommates – one black, one white (who I will refer to as Alma and Sarah to respect their privacy).

Alma, my black roommate, was a friend and colleague. As high school seniors, Alma and I had been youth organizers in the fair housing melee in Louisville, Kentucky. During those moments in history, all part of the twentieth-century civil rights movement, Alma and I were swept along in the crosshairs of the fight for equal opportunity for all people. We were part of the Youth Brigade which marched on city hall. Our sit-in in the chambers led to our being part of the mass arrest of teenagers who were at the forefront of the protests.

All of this activity was part of the now famous historical anti-redlining housing desegregation movement which, in part, led to the passage of the Fair Housing Act of 1968. The Fair Housing Campaign was led by Uncle ML. The winning strategy of the Kentucky-based operations for the movement was led by my dad, Reverend Alfred Daniel Williams King. Daddy was the pastor of

Zion Baptist Church in Louisville and founder of the Kentucky Christian Leadership Conference (KCLC). KCLC was a subsidiary of the Southern Christian Leadership Conference (SCLC) headed by Uncle ML. In fact, the Fair Housing Act was passed just days after my uncle was shot.

It was also during those days that I crossed onto a very dangerous path of embracing hate rather than the love my uncle and my dad taught us to embrace during their lifetimes. It was during those days when Uncle ML was shot that I told my daddy I hated white people. Daddy wouldn't accept my bitter diatribe. Wrapping his arms around me in our kitchen in Kentucky on that night Uncle ML was shot, Daddy told me, "White people didn't kill your Uncle ML. White people live with us, pray with us, march with us, and die with us. White people didn't kill my brother. The devil did."

Daddy traveled by private jet to get Aunt Coretta and escort her to Memphis where they would pick up Uncle ML's body and bring it to Atlanta.

While it would be a long and painful journey to completely embrace the truth of Daddy's words, it was the love of my daddy, and ultimately my heavenly Father, that carried me through the days ahead. That message of eternal love and forgiveness still reverberates in my heart even as this book is being written.

It wasn't long after Uncle ML's death and the passage of the Fair Housing Act that I went away to college and met Sarah. She was such a bright, pretty, and compassionate person. Since Sarah, Alma, and I were roommates, we spent many of our evenings talking about the days and times of our lives. Sarah wanted to empathize with Alma and me when we would talk about the Movement and the death of Uncle ML.

One evening during such a conversation, something came over me. It would be easy to just say it was the devil. Please bear with me while I try to explain the situation in more depth. Sarah was speaking to Alma and me, trying to express remorse about what we as black women had experienced and lost. For some reason, the bitterness I tried to repress over the past few months just welled up inside of me. I yelled at Sarah with something like, "Shut up. What do you know about it? You're white, you're privileged, and you just don't care. I hate white people!"

I can still see Sarah's face today, flushed and marred with tears streaming down her face. She was a pretty girl back then, bright and happy, until my words changed all of that. It is important to describe Sarah because, after all, as the title of this book explains, I wasn't colorblind then. I'm not colorblind now. I saw Sarah's pink face, fair hair, and clear watery tears, and I didn't care how hurt she was back then. I was angry and bitter. I was hurting, too. I think I broke her heart, though I hope not forever. I pray that Sarah forgives me. She was such a lovely soul.

We never talked again after those days. At the end of the semester, Alma left school. Sarah requested a new roommate. I was assigned to my own room. There, in much solitude, I stewed in my own bitter juices for the next few months. Somehow, a decision was made for me to return home and marry my high school sweetheart at the end of my freshman year. With Uncle ML now gone, Daddy and Mama returned to Atlanta where Daddy would take over Uncle ML's post as co-pastor with Granddaddy, Reverend Martin Luther King Sr.

It was during those days of sadness and loss that Daddy and Granddaddy, with love and hope in their hearts, continued to preach the Gospel of Jesus Christ. They carried the good news that we are created in the image and likeness of God and that we are the one blood and one human race of Acts 17:26. They understood that we would have to accept that we are not separate races but are one race, the human race. They held strong to the belief that we can learn to live together as brothers and sisters and not perish as fools. Though I couldn't express it at the time, it was refreshing that this truth didn't die with Uncle ML. Many years would pass before I would embrace their legacy and learn to live and teach these truths.

At the turn of the twenty-first century, I began to think about those early days. I mourned not having apologized to Sarah for the injury my judgments against her had caused.

I began to wish that I could find Sarah and apologize. Little did I know that God would give me another chance at reconciliation with a new Sarah in the form of a woman named Ginger Howard. I would once again have a chance to learn to live together with a friend as her sister, where we would not be colorblind but would proclaim truth in living color.

Of course, there have been many reconciled and lasting friendships forged across the color spectrum over the years following that misguided skin color breach I expressed toward Sarah. I hurt her deeply. I am still so sorry. I believe God has forgiven me. I pray that

Sarah has, wherever she may be. Having been born again in Christ, I have a new and repentant heart.

Many years have passed, many hurts and hearts have been healed. While Ginger isn't my first true friend from another ethnic group, it's still clear that, in these present days and times, God wants to use multiethnic relationships as shining examples of the truth of Acts 17:26. As human beings, we are one blood and one race. We have the ability to learn to live together as brothers and sisters so that we won't perish together as fools.

Graciously, God has been very specific regarding my relationship with Ginger. God means for Ginger and me to see each other in the beautiful "living color" that He created for each of us. In my eyes, Ginger is petite with blond hair. Her coloring is much like Sarah's was. Her skin color is fair, not white. Though there are distinct differences in our physical appearance, what Ginger and I share in common is much more significant and truer. We both love shopping for vintage treasures and share an appreciation for "dramatic flair" in our wardrobe. We both enjoy art, music, and flowers. Of greater importance, we share a passion for moral, social, and economic justice. We both lead very busy lives, but when time allows, we get together to savor the joys of life.

Teachable moment: No human being has skin that is literally black or white unless something is terribly wrong. All of us humans have color in our skin tones; some more, and some less, depending on the amount of melanin we are allocated. Melanin is the pigment that gives human skin, hair, and eyes their color. Dark-skinned people have more melanin in their skin than light-skinned people have.

Melanin is produced by cells called melanocytes. It provides some protection against skin damage from the sun, and the melanocytes increase their production of melanin in response to sun exposure. Freckles, which occur in people of all races, are small, concentrated areas of increased melanin production. The amount of melanin allocated to people groups does not determine their race. As Acts 17:26 accurately describes, we are of one blood, one human race.

When Ginger and I first met, we accepted each other as sisters in Christ. As such, we have been able to reach far beyond any skin-color boundaries. We recognized and realized that God had something very special in store for the two of us. For me, it's almost like God was rolling back my reality-check clock to the 1960s, and I was back with Sarah. God was tugging on my heartstrings and once again whispering "reconcile" in my ear. This time I was ready to hear and obey.

Reflection: What secrets are tucked away in your heart that you can bring to the light?

—PRAYER—

Dear Heavenly Father, the Bible teaches us that we can hide Your Word in our hearts so that we won't sin against You. Please teach us how to bring more of Your Word into our hearts and lives. In Jesus's name, Amen.

That their hearts may be encouraged,
being knit together in love. . . .

—Colossians 2:2 NKJV—

Ginger Speaks

In April of 2018, ten days after I spoke at the Martin Luther King Jr. Commemorative Service at Ebenezer Baptist Church, I dreamed that Alveda and I wrote a book about racial reconciliation. I had the dream on a Wednesday night, and I left Alveda a message the following day, asking her to call me back. I shared the dream with her that Saturday, and we prayed together. Six hours later, she sent me the book title and the outline. I knew this was from God.

There are many reasons I am an unlikely person to be writing this book with the niece of a civil rights leader like Martin Luther King Jr. I am a white woman who was born in South Georgia during the height of the civil rights movement. Since my community was largely segregated, it wasn't until recently that the racial divisions in our country have become a burden to me. I am thankful that the Lord has opened my eyes to an area in our nation that needs deep healing and that He has put it on my heart to be part of the solution through partnering with my sister, Alveda.

We are coming together to address this sensitive topic and continue the dialogue. And, while I am hopeful about the ways Alveda and I contribute to conversations around race, I am not naïve enough to think that one book on racial reconciliation will fix the deep divisions in our country.

I have never written a book before, although it has been a dream of mine for many years. I also never imagined that my first book would be about racial reconciliation nor that I would write it with Dr. Alveda King, who is a best-selling author! But, that is how God works. He never calls the qualified; He qualifies the called. He called me to write this book, and He had to show me in a dream. It is so like God to give me a literal dream when over fifty years ago He gave Alveda's uncle, Dr. Martin Luther King Jr., a dream that one day sons and daughters of former slave owners and sons and daughters of former slaves would sit down at the table of brotherly love.

One day Alveda came to my house for lunch with my dear friend and mentor, Ann Platz Groton. Her ancestors were actually a part of the slave trade. Here are her own words:

"My name is Ann Platz Groton. I live in Atlanta, Georgia. I am a champion of racial reconciliation. However, some of my maternal family's distant ancestors were wealthy slave owners in Charleston, South Carolina, in the late 1600s.

"When I started doing research for my novel *The Inheritance Riddle*, I discovered that Charleston had been saturated with slaves brought in from the large Low Country rice plantations. These Senegalese people had been sold into slavery by their own people—their kings. These slaves ended up in Charleston because Senegal was the closest port to the colony of Charles Town.

As I learned more about the slave trade, I was shocked to read about the conditions these people endured, and even more shocked to discover that one of my direct forebears had been the leading slave trader in the American colonies in the late 1600s.

Of course, neither I nor any of my recent ancestors had been involved in or sympathized with this kind of nefarious activity, but I felt a strong desire to expunge any remaining taint from my family's former connection with slavery.

Nevertheless, feeling a sense of shame about my ancestors, I made an appointment to visit the Senegalese Embassy in Washington. I met with the gentleman in charge and explained my interest in Senegal and the need to repent for my family's involvement in slavery. It was a moving experience when the Senegalese gentleman accepted and joined in my prayer for forgiveness.

During the past few generations, distinguished members from both sides of my family have served in high-level government positions. Each of them served with honor and embraced racial reconciliation. In fact, some of them actively assisted in integrating the South Carolina schools.

I have long admired Dr. King's courage and his message, and I have championed his great successes. I hope this above testimony will be of help in understanding the need to improve race relations."

I include Ann's story to demonstrate that the three of us ate at the table of sisterly love. Fifty years ago, that was only a dream, but today it is reality because of how Dr. Martin Luther King Jr. and many others paved the way for us to have a meeting of the hearts.

I first heard Alveda speak at a pro-life dinner where she shared about the regret and pain resulting from her abortions and gave her testimony about later becoming a born-again believer in the Lord. I was very moved by her story. I was so impacted by that night that I participated in my first March for Life rally at the Georgia State Capitol. I also lobbied my state senator for pro-life laws. Later on, I had Alveda on a radio show called the Freedom Five that I hosted with four other Christian conservative women to discuss her stance on the life of the unborn.

Our paths would cross at other times, as they did one day when we flew on the same plane to and from Washington, D.C. Our hearts really bonded in August of 2017 when we were a part of the Beloved Community Talks panel on racial reconciliation at the King Center. We will discuss that in a later chapter.

Alveda and I both share the same love and heart for our Lord Jesus. We both believe His Word is the infallible Word of God and that His heart has brought us together for such a time as this. Our nation is divided in so many ways, not just with race but also with politics, religion, gender, and so on. We believe Jesus gave us the ministry of reconciliation and, without Him, there is no reconciliation. (See 2 Corinthians 5:18.)

My prayer for this book is that all who read it will see in Alveda and me the heart of Jesus for our country and for our brothers and sisters of all ethnicities and cultures. We both love this nation and have a heart that it truly be one nation under God. We want to live in unity and harmony with everyone, celebrate our different cultures, and recognize the fact that we all came from one Creator who created us in His image to be His image-bearers.

I pray that this book will begin a new phase of this conversation which will grow and begin to heal the divide that has too many of us on opposite sides of one another. I pray that everyone who reads this book would feel the compassion and love Alveda and I feel for you and each other and that our hearts would meet even if we never meet you personally. I pray you would feel a connection to us here on these pages as we share our hearts.

Reflection: Have you missed an opportunity to build a bridge along the way? Is there a window of opportunity open for you now to make a difference regarding relations with diverse people groups in the world today?

—PRAYER—

Dear Heavenly Father, thank You for Your heart for us. Thank You that we love because You first loved us. Lord, I pray for every person who is reading this book, that their hearts would be stirred by the power of Your love, and that You would stir all of us to have a deep love for our brothers and sisters of all ethnicities and cultures. Knit our hearts together as only You can. In Jesus's name, Amen.

Chapter Two

A MEETING OF THE MINDS

---◉---

*Fulfill my joy by being like-minded, having the
same love, being of one accord, of one mind.*

—Philippians 2:2 NKJV—

---◉---

Ginger Speaks

The above Scripture is relevant for the topic of racial reconciliation, but it also holds special significance for me since the
Lord highlighted this verse for me to pray over Alveda and myself
as we coauthor this book. And, as God always does, He answered
exceedingly abundantly above all I asked or imagined.

I stole away one weekend to find some quiet space to reflect and
write, and that same morning, I received a text from Alveda saying
she was praying for me. In the text, she included this Bible verse,
"My heart is stirred by a noble theme as I recite my verses for the

king; my tongue is the pen of a skillful writer" (Psalm 45:1, NIV). Her words filled me with such gratitude for the friendship and one-ness that God is faithfully cultivating between us.

Alveda is a skilled writer and has authored several books, and the fact that she had confidence in me to write this book with her is a gift from God Himself. She took a chance with me because she believes God works through anyone who is obedient to His call. She also believes in prophetic dreams and, since the idea for this book was birthed in a dream, she was open to making the dream come true. Her grandfather had a dream about her before she was born, but I will let her share that story.

I am writing this chapter from Barnsley Gardens, a beautiful resort in Adairsville, which is an hour north of Atlanta. When I chose to come here for the weekend, I didn't know anything about the history of the resort, but God knew. I checked in and, since my room was not ready, the desk clerk suggested I take a golf cart tour of the gardens. My host drove me to see the ruins of the home of Godfrey and Julia Barnsley. On the tour, he pointed out the very steps where Margaret Mitchell supposedly sat to get inspiration for her novel *Gone with the Wind*.

Godfrey Barnsley was an Englishman and wealthy cotton mer-chant. He began construction on the home for his wife, Julia, in 1828. She, unfortunately, died before the house was finished, leav-ing behind her beloved husband and six children.

Godfrey was from England and didn't believe in slavery, so when he married Julia and inherited seven slaves, he made them servants instead. Their family estate was spared by General Sherman in the

Civil War, and Godfrey's daughter Julia, carrying on the namesake of her mother, fought hard to restore and preserve their land after the fighting ended.

In the 1920s, Margaret Mitchell frequented the home to spend time with Julia's daughter, Addie, to learn more about her family history. Julia became the inspiration for Scarlett O'Hara, the leading character in Mitchell's *Gone with the Wind*, which is one of the most famous books on southern culture post-Civil War.[1]

I find it not by accident that God had planned for me to start this book in a place that has deep roots in the Civil War and the racially segregated south. Of all the places I could have gone this weekend in March, I believe God had me come to Barnsley Gardens to write about racial reconciliation and, in doing so, to reclaim the land, spiritually speaking. God is in the restoration business. Nothing is by chance.

Although the Civil War ended in the spring of 1865, it took almost one hundred years for the Civil Rights Act of 1965 to pass. The year of the writing of this book marks the fiftieth anniversary of the assassination of Alveda's uncle, Dr. Martin Luther King, Jr., who was one of the leaders of the civil rights movement. He believed in a day where people would not judge others by the color of their skin but rather by the content of their character.

We have lived to see the day where an African American man was elected president, but we still have miles to go in truly living together as brothers and sisters. One of Dr. Martin Luther King Jr.'s most memorable quotes was, "We must learn to live together as brothers or perish together as fools." Some days, it seems as though we are perishing as fools. How can we learn to live together as one people, unified in love for each other? We don't have to agree about everything, but we can grow to value each other's perspectives while still pursuing harmony.

The nonviolent movement that Dr. Martin Luther King Jr. initiated was founded on Biblical principles. He was a Baptist minister and embodied the love of Christ. He said, "Nonviolence is absolute commitment to the way of love. Love is not emotional bash; it is not empty sentimentalism. It is the active outpouring of one's whole being into the being of one another."[2]

I realize not everyone reading this book has a relationship with Jesus as their Savior. But it is my prayer and desire, as I know it is Alveda's, that if you do not have a personal relationship with God the Father through His Son Jesus Christ, by the end of this book you will make that life-changing choice to make Jesus your Lord and Savior. Every other religion is based on works and trying to get *to God*, but Christianity is God coming down *to us*, not based on any performance. We don't do anything to deserve His grace, but in His mercy, He loved us so much that He sent Jesus to reconcile us to Himself.

John 3:16–18 puts it this way, "This is how much God loved the world: He gave his Son, his one and only Son. And this is why: so that no one need be destroyed; by believing in him, anyone can have a whole and lasting life. God didn't go to all the trouble of sending his Son merely to point an accusing finger, telling the world how bad it was. He came to help, to put the world right again. Anyone who trusts in him is acquitted; anyone who refuses to trust him has long since been under the death sentence without knowing it. And why? Because of that person's failure to believe in the one-of-a-kind Son of God when introduced to him" (MSG).

Now, you may be asking yourself, "What does this have to do with racial reconciliation?" Well, it has everything to do with it because Jesus Himself gave us the ministry of reconciliation. 2 Corinthians 5:18–23 says, "All this is from God, who reconciled us to himself through Christ and gave us the ministry of reconciliation; that God was reconciling the world to himself in Christ, not counting men's sins against them. And he has committed to us the message of reconciliation. We are therefore Christ's ambassadors, as though God were making his appeal through us. We implore you on Christ's behalf: Be reconciled to God. God made him who had no sin to be sin for us, so that in him we might become the righteousness of God" (NIV).

Reconciliation is defined as "the restoration of friendly relations; the action of making one view or belief compatible with another."[2] Because we have been restored to friendship with God, and we are His children, the legacy of reconciliation runs in our blood. Being a Christian literally means "to be a little Christ,"[4] and so we have been given the charge of restoring friendly relations and fostering compatibility between different types of people. God's heart is for us to be reconciled to Him and for us to be reconciled to each other. He used Jesus as the perfect model for reconciliation; we were divided and separated from Him because of our sins, so He sent His Son Jesus as a perfect sacrifice to unite us back to God.

In order for true reconciliation to take place, we have to see ourselves and others as Jesus does. Essentially, since Jesus is the ultimate Reconciler, we need to take on His perspective and His thoughts on the subject. According to Scripture, believers have been given the mind of Christ so that we are able to fulfill the command in Philippians 2:2, "Fulfill my joy by being like-minded, having the same love, being of one accord, of one mind" (NIV). And, as Paul references in this verse, there is joy fulfilled when unity and oneness take place.

Sadly, the church as a whole has not embraced the mind of Christ when it comes to the ministry of reconciliation. There is much room for improvement in mending broken relationships and healing divisions in our country. However, we can learn a great deal from Dr. Martin Luther King Jr. in the ways he modeled God's heart for reconciliation even in the most extreme circumstances. We have the opportunity to carry on the torch he left behind.

Reflection: How have you seen reconciliation take place between people of different backgrounds? What is one step that you can take towards seeing someone different than you with the same eyes that Jesus has?

—PRAYER—

Dear Heavenly Father, thank You for giving us the mind of Christ on reconciliation. You taught us how to reconcile by sending Your Son to die a sinner's death so that we may have reconciliation with You. I pray for the ministry of reconciliation between people from various ethnic and cultural backgrounds, Lord. Help us have Your mind, and love with Your love. Use us to be Your hands and feet and show the love of Christ. Lord, reveal Your mind to us and give us Your heart to heal our divisions. In Jesus's name, Amen.

━━━━━◉━━━━━

*To the chief Musician upon Shoshannim, for the sons
of Korah, Mashil, a song of loves. My heart is inditing
a good matter: I speak of the things which I have made
touching the king: my tongue is the pen of a ready writer.*

—Psalm 45:1 KJV—

Let this mind be in you which was also in Christ Jesus.

—Philippians 2:5 KJV—

━━━━━◉━━━━━

Alveda Speaks

When Ginger first spoke to me about her dream for this book, my spirit was moved quickly into agreement with the concept. At that time and in regards to the project, the first Scripture that came to mind was Psalm 45:1. This is the same Scripture that Ginger writes about in the beginning of this chapter. Ginger and I are indeed "ready writers" having the same mind and the same heart for reconciling diverse people into communities of mutual love, respect, and unity. We share the mind of Christ.

As I'm writing this chapter, I find myself wondering if Holy Spirit whispers this ready-writer Scripture to those inspired to write poetry, books, letters, and all types of messages. This Scripture also comes to mind:

> But the anointing which you have received from him abides in you, and you do not need that anyone teach you.

49

But as his anointing teaches you concerning all things, and is true and is not a lie, and just as it has taught you, you abide in Him (1 John 2:27 NKJV).

While Ginger and I write from a Christian worldview, we both agree that racial reconciliation should be a goal for every human being. We use Christian examples as references because we are unabashedly Christian—no apologies needed. However, we have a goal to reach the hearts and minds of our readers with the examples and anecdotes regarding racial unity that will reach into your own life experiences and invite you to think and rethink the subject of race-related issues.

I have a favorite saying, "Where peripherals collide, convergence is imminent." On the surface, Ginger and I have totally diverse life-styles; socially, physically, economically, and philosophically. We brush into each other in the fringes, so to speak. However, our spiritual convergence is awesome. We have become "spiritual sisters in the human experience."

Along the way, as you progress through the chapters, you will notice a common theme. We are one blood/one human race. Any references to the old concept of us being separate races are the result of old habits dying hard. Even if you accept the reality of being a part of "one blood/one human race," you may have the challenge of making the "mental and spiritual paradigm shift" to thinking, speaking, and living as belonging to "one blood/one race." That's okay. Don't sweat it. Transformation takes time.

Earlier in the chapter, Ginger wrote of her sojourn to the estate of abolitionist Godfrey Barnsley. It was there that she wrote her portion of this chapter. I'm sitting in a quiet hotel in Michigan writing my part of the chapter. It's amazing how God unites the hearts, minds, and thoughts of two women from diverse backgrounds to deliver a message for such a time as this.

Even as Ginger wrote of the English abolitionist Godfrey Barnsley, who reportedly inspired Margaret Mitchell's epic classic, *Gone with the Wind*, my thoughts and keystrokes turn to another abolitionist, the first Duke of Sussex. Prince Augustus Frederick, the sixth son of King George III and uncle of Queen Victoria, was awarded the title of Duke of Sussex in 1801.[5] He was a supporter of the abolition of the slave trade and expressed disregard for the legal restrictions placed on Jews.

Amazingly, over one hundred years later, in 2018, the second Duke of Sussex was appointed. Prince Harry of England and his bride, Meghan Markle, received the honor and titles of Duke and Duchess of Sussex from Harry's grandmother Queen Elizabeth on their wedding day, May 19, 2018. Meghan Markle is the second ethnically blended person to be publicly recognized as a member of the Royal Family.

Note that we say "ethnically blended" rather than bi-racial since the Duchess is a member of the one-blood human race. Though there are different blood types, there is only one human blood design and one color – red. There is no such thing as bi-racial. There are no bi-racial people. There are no bi-racial marriages. Just as the love of money is the root of all evil (1 Timothy 6:10), the lie of separate races is the root of many evils. It is important to emphasize here that it is the *love* of money that is the root of all evil. Money by itself is not evil; covetousness and obsession with money is the root of all evil. Skin color is not evil; racial division over skin color is the root of much evil. This information could lead us to wonder if the love of money and debates over skin color are connected in some way. We will leave that question for another chapter. Further exploration of the question will lead us to long even more deeply for racial reconciliation. For now, I want to continue sharing how this moment in the Royal Family of England has breathed new life in our efforts toward ethnic and cultural unity.

The reality of people of different ethnic backgrounds being members of the Royal Family of England is not new. In the eighteenth century, Queen Sophie Charlotte was the first known black queen of England. She was born on May 19, 1744.[6] She became Queen Sophie Charlotte, wife of King George III, and bore the king fifteen children. Queen Sophie was of African descent, allegedly directly descended from a black branch of the Portuguese royal family (Alfonso III and his concubine, Ouruana, a black Moor).

Queen Charlotte reigned for sixty years.[7] In many historic portraits, her features were white-washed with paint to conceal her African ancestry. This practice, akin to disfiguring images such as the Sphinx and Roman coinage, became common by the nineteenth century for many other portraits of famous black people throughout Europe and Asia.[8]

Queen Sophie Charlotte's birthday, May 19, not so coincidentally coincides with the date Duke Harry, Duchess Meghan, and the Royal Family—May 19, 2018—chose as the wedding date for another black woman to be married into the Royal Family.

As the world watched the marriage union of Prince Harry and Meghan Markle in May of 2018, the winds of racial reconciliation were blowing across the nations. These occurrences are in keeping with the dream of my Uncle ML. He, too, had a dream of racial reconciliation, of one blood united. Uncle ML, my father, and my grandfather often preached of one blood using Acts 17:26 as the foundation.

Even the marriage of Duke Harry and Duchess Meghan are examples of the Acts 17:26 principle. God's voice was heard at their wedding in the message of love proclaimed by Bishop Curry. It would be very hard to deny the overtones of racial reconciliation that permeated the occasion. Perhaps we can all take a page from their book and move ahead as one blood.

As founder of the Reconciled Church, Bishop Harry Jackson leads a successful movement for racial and spiritual reconciliation in the twenty-first century. He believes that "we can shift the racial atmosphere of the nation by healing the racial divisions in the church." On his website, Bishop Jackson writes, "Healing the racial divide in the nation will take the Church's leadership. More specifically, we will need specific steps of action to heal the nation by engaging in the seven spheres of activity. We strongly believe that if the Church takes unified action in real time, we can avert a national crisis and restore a sense of purpose and destiny to many individuals, their churches, and their communities. The root problems of America's ghettos are not unlike the problems of the nation's suburbs. Strangely enough, participating in the strategies that will bring a sense of justice to urban America will revitalize the Christian experience and devotion of suburban and affluent Christians as well."

Bishop Jackson and other like-minded people are on to an important truth. Having the mind of Christ for racial reconciliation is a good step in the right direction for solving the age-old problem of racism. We can all join in the racial reconciliation movement.

One way to do this is to stop referring to ourselves as separate races according to our skin color. My race as a brown-skinned woman is human. Ginger's race as a peaches-and-cream skin-colored woman is human. The color of our skin does not denote our race; our red blood does. We all bleed the same. Can we stop referring to ourselves as separate races because of skin color? Ginger and I have, and we are not colorblind.

Reflection: Ask yourself this question: "What can I do to help bring about racial reconciliation?"

—PRAYER—

Dear Heavenly Father, in Your Word, Jesus prayed that we all may be one. He also prayed that people will know we are Christ's disciples when we live out our love for each other. Lord, we pray today for more faith, love, and action for reconciliation, not just for skin color but for our hearts. In Jesus's name, Amen.

Chapter Three

POLITICS ASIDE

---◉---

When the righteous are in authority,
the people rejoice, but when a wicked man rules,
the people groan.

—Proverbs 29:2 NKJV—

You nullify the word of God by your tradition
that you have handed down.
And you do many things like that.

—Mark 7:13 NIV—

Don't be misled—
you cannot mock the justice of God.
You will always harvest what you plant.

—Galatians 6:7 NLT—

---◉---

Don't tell me that money is the root of all evil. That may be so. Sometimes I feel that the White man, knowing that Blacks (having no want to be evil) would believe the myth that the possession of money can cause evil deeds.

However, lack of money causes many more evil situations, like the little children with sagging skin and swollen bellies; families living in matchbox houses, literal fire traps; victims of poverty forced to steal because they feel there is no other way out.

Yes, I like money. Not only because it can buy things for me, but because one day, if I get enough money, I can help others.

There is one class in our society who thinks more about money than the rich, and they are the poor. They can think of nothing else, which is the misery of being poor. Poverty produces degradation.

For me, money will always be an instrument to be handled, a weapon to fight poverty – not a deity to be worshiped.

—Dr. Alveda King

Alveda Speaks

It seems as though I've spent quite a bit of my life either running from politics or running into politics. As a young woman growing up in the 1960s and 1970s, I wasn't quite sure what I was looking for, or why I thought that I'd find my answers in the political realm. I only knew that something was wrong in the world and that I wanted to help make things better, make things right. So, I began to play the political game.

As a Democrat in the 1970s, I volunteered for various campaigns, starting at the mayoral level. I moved into the congressional field and finally into the organizational team of a presidential campaign. After that, I ran for office myself as a Democrat and won a House seat in the Georgia Legislature.

It was only after I was born again in 1983 that I realized politics could never be the ultimate go-to for solutions to the human condition. Yet, I wasn't quite ready to abandon the political realm in favor of seeking only the divine path. I continued to engage in politics from a "different side of the aisle."

In the early 1990s, realizing that I could no longer support their agenda which included abortion and the weakening of the natural family, I walked away from the Democrat Party and became an Independent for several years. Then, in the late 1990s, in support of the Pro-life platform and the Religious Freedom agenda, I became a Frederick Douglass Republican. Since that time, I have received two presidential appointments.

While I was in the position of being a "Frederick Douglass Republican" in 2008, God laid it on my heart to "stop endorsing candidates and start praying." As a result, there have been no more political endorsements from me. However, I have since become a "spiritual advisor" to certain candidates who have sought my support. In this role, I participate in prayer sessions, and prayer rallies. More importantly, I have finally come to understand that politics can never be the end-all to the fulfillment of human desires.

My Uncle ML once said, "Morality cannot be legislated, but behavior can be regulated. Judicial decrees may not change the heart, but they can restrain the heartless." I've paraphrased his words so many times, often reminding people that we can't legislate morality. While laws can restrain human misconduct to some degree, only God can transform the human heart to a state where inhumane deeds will diminish among humanity.

If this premise is true, then, I've often wondered, why do so many people spend more time discussing politics than they spend praying or just unwinding with friends and family? Strangely, while many go about the everyday routines of life, a grim phenomenon has consistently grown, threatening to destroy the moral and social fiber of our nation and the world. Politics and the traditions of humans have increasingly become idols.

Mark 7:13 says,

"You nullify the word of God by your tradition that you have handed down. And you do many things like that." (NIV)

During the 2015 political elections in the United States, the nation was divided between two political parties and two presidential candidates. Leading up to the general elections, the Republican Party waged a contentious contest that began with seventeen candidates on the ballot. In the end, the man least expected to win took the prize.

The run for the Democratic ticket was not nearly so contentiously carried out. Victory seemed to be assured for Mrs. Hillary Clinton, the winner of that contest. Yet, nothing went as planned or expected. President Donald John Trump became the forty-fifth President of the United States of America.

In 2018, as I began to write this chapter, political mayhem was having a party. Everything was part of a devious game. There were many critical domestic and international topics that were being kicked around like footballs in a political game — including the sanctity of life, fair and decent education for all, and the value of the human personality regardless of skin color and socioeconomic status.

In 2019 under the then current presidential administration, there were certain upward shifts in the economy, religious freedom, criminal justice and the broader social strata. These shifts encouraged more prayers for America to return to God. As a result, praying for all in authority became more and more a focus for me.

Often, some politicians seem to join in debates without really being emotionally or spiritually committed to the cause. They use issues like pawns in a political game of chess in order to win a seat or a position, not truly caring about the cause. Therefore, it often becomes the responsibility of the voters to rally troops for the battles. This is an assignment that many like me take seriously.

Here in the 21st century, I'm mostly known for my ministry in the area of anti-abortion and the sanctity of life. I first became a voice for life in 1983 when I was born again.

It was at the turn of the century that I met Reverend Frank Pavone. He is the national director of Priests for Life. I met him at a National Right to Life meeting in New York, and we became friends over a period of time as our paths continued to cross.

Later, I accepted a ministerial assignment to head up the civil rights program at Priests for Life, now at www.civilrightsforth-eunborn.org, where we confront the injustice of abortion and speak out for the sanctity of life.

My battle for the sanctity of life began in my mother's womb. I was born on January 22, 1951. My very birth was a miracle and a testament to the sanctity of life in that in 1950, spurred on by propaganda of "The Birth Control League" which would become well known as today's "Planned Parenthood," my mother wanted to have a D&C (Dilation and Curettage) procedure to end her pregnancy. Thank God, my grandfather, Rev. Martin Luther King, Sr., convinced her to keep me. [Historical note: The names Martin Luther King, Sr. and Martin Luther King, Jr. were changed from Michael Luther King to Martin Luther King by my grandfather in honor of his mother, and in recognition of the famous reformer Martin Luther.]

Granddaddy insisted that he had seen me in a prophetic dream three years before my birth, and he described me "to a tee." I was born to my loving parents Alfred Daniel Williams King and Naomi Ruth Barber King on January 22, 1951.

Twenty-two years after my birth, the controversial abortion case Roe vs. Wade made the abortion of babies in the womb legal.

Ironically, while I had been protected from being aborted in 1950, years later, after Roe vs. Wade became law, I became pro-choice and even suffered two secret abortions and a miscarriage during that time.

Years later, I accepted Christ as my Savior, and I became pro-life. Time passed, and in 2018 I became an Executive Producer for a new Roe V. Wade movie. Wow. Talk about how peripherals collide and imminently converge!

Understanding the obvious parallels in my life, I have often said that part of my mission and one of the reasons that I'm alive, is to protect human life at all stages.

The ministry of protecting the sanctity of life at all stages is not a political game. The mission is more like a war. During these trying times, America is akin to a polarized battlefield. Everyone is either for or against something. The world of politics is usually at the center of the battle. There is something very wrong with this picture.

The 45th President of the United States reintroduced prayer and faith as part of his agenda. "In America we do not worship government, we worship God," he has declared. His stance is in keeping with America returning to God.

This perspective brings America closer to the reality that we have more in common than we realize. Here in nearly the third decade of the 21st century, regardless of skin color, an unprecedented lower unemployment rate impacts our communities for a common good. A lower abortion rate is a moral and civil rights victory for every baby that is saved. These victories are opportunities for Americans to see each other as human beings with common goals and needs.

"Don't be misled—you cannot mock the justice of God. You will always harvest what you plant" (Galatians 6:7 NLT).

Consequently, we must always beware and must not ever allow a president or any human leader to become an idol in our ideology. We would be wise to admit that human leaders cannot save America; and we cannot either.

Working through us, only God can bless and save America. To that end, natural law—God's law—will always trump common law. Do not fear or be confused or deceived. Remain prayerful. Keep looking up. God will have the final word in this matter.

I must admit that learning to give God the final word in my own political sphere is sometimes still a difficult commitment. Having been born into a family of freedom fighters and justice seekers from a generational pool that bridged three continents—Africa, Ireland, and pre-colonized America—I was born with both faith and politics in my blood.

My grandfather's (Reverend Martin Luther King, Sr.) grandfather, Nathan Branham King, was an Irish freedom fighter. My grandmother's (Alberta Williams King) grandfather, Willis Williams, was a freed slave and a preacher. My mother's (Naomi Ruth Barber King) father, Square Reese, was reported to be from the Cherokee Nation in America. The King branch (or bloodline) is connected to the Irish diaspora. The Williams branch (or bloodline) is connected to the abolitionist (antislavery) movement in America. The injustice to both the Irish and African nations, as well as the Native American nations, is well documented in the annals of America's history.

It is the political and faith-based journeys shared in communal trials and triumphs among these three nations that are often at the core of the political and spiritual foundations that are under attack, even in the twenty-first century.

Over the years, our family has always talked openly about life and culture in different lands. Skin color is never an issue or an opportunity for division in our conversations. Differences and diversity are seen as interesting human assets to be celebrated and respected.

I was raised to love people as people according to John 3:16; equally and unconditionally. This may be a difficult premise to accept, but the people of America and around the world might be well served to take a step back from political bickering and learn to love each other as brothers and sisters – and fellow human beings.

"We must learn to live together as brothers [and sisters] and not perish together as fools." The Prophet Martin Luther King, Jr.

So, if we are not to perish as a nation or as the human race, we must learn to learn to live together. We must also acknowledge that the realm of political governance remains an integral part of human life.

Even Jesus said, 'Give unto Caesar what is Caesar's, and to God what belongs to God.'

Yet it remains important to also acknowledge that it is God and not political voices who will have the final say in the judgment of humanity. The United States Supreme Court is the highest court in America and rules from a position of common law—human law. Yet there is a higher court, the court of heaven where God presides. In the final analysis, God's court rules with the law that really matters. God's law will always trump human politics.

Before his transition to heaven, our pastor Allen McNair once taught us, "Don't vote for sin." I took that lesson to heart. As a result, I continue to raise up the banner of love and vote for life.

I stay in the fight praying and voting for life and family for generations to come. I will continue to pray for and to vote for life, liberty and justice for everyone; the child in the womb, the person behind bars, the poor, the sick, the elderly, the enslaved and the free. I pray and vote for economic, social and moral justice for everyone; for safety and security for everyone.

Here is where politics submits to God. We must always serve God, not just at church on Sundays. We must also pray and serve God at the polls.

> If My people who are called by My name will humble themselves, and pray and seek My face, and turn from their wicked ways, then I will hear from heaven, and will forgive their sin and heal their land (2 Chronicles 7:14 NKJV).

Pray this way for kings and all who are in authority so that we can live peaceful and quiet lives marked by godliness and dignity (1 Timothy 2:2 NLT).

Along with these Scriptures above, I cite as a foundation Scripture throughout this book,

'From one blood GOD created all humanity throughout the whole earth. GOD decided beforehand when they should rise and fall, and GOD determined their boundaries. "GOD'S purpose was for the nations to seek after God and perhaps feel their way toward GOD and find GOD —though GOD is not far from any one of us. For in GOD we live and move and exist. As some of your own poets have said, 'We are GOD'S offspring" (Acts 17:26-28 Paraphrased from NLT).

We can see above that the Bible teaches us that GOD created all of us of one blood. We are one human race. So, every nation, every tongue, every tribe is still one human race. It is this scriptural foundation that guides me as I navigate the political seasons.

[A little known secret: During my lifetime, I have had the honor of being invited to the White House during the administrations of at least six presidents of the United States of America for various reasons, agendas, and purposes.]

I didn't always have a spiritual perspective about politics. As a member of the Georgia Legislature from 1978–1982, I was more "political" than "spiritual." While that was a successful season in my life, awakening and transformation were further down the road.

When I became a born-again Christian in 1983, my perspective slowly shifted from political to spiritual and this focus remains in my heart today.

The prayer perspective is that all votes matter. Whether you're a Christian or not a Christian, religious or not religious, and whether you are red, yellow, black, or white, our blood is red.

In his inaugural speech, President Donald John Trump said, "We all bleed the same." I remember saying that day, "Wow. He gets it." He has also said, "We don't worship government. We worship God." That's true.

So, when worshiping God, and praying, and considering all the candidates, if you're in America, no matter who you vote for, remember, it's all about seeking reconciliation.

As Americans, "We all bleed the same."

In context with our quest for seeking racial reconciliation, it should be appropriate and acceptable to discuss the impact of racism on the voting rights of African Americans in this chapter.

Uncle MLK once gave a compelling speech on the subject:

"GIVE US THE BALLOT"

"Give us the ballot and we will no longer have to worry the government about our basic rights. Give us the ballot and we will no longer plead to the federal government for passage of an anti-lynching law ... Give us the ballot and we will fill our legislative halls with men of good will ...

Give us the ballot and we will place judges on the benches of the South who will do justly and love mercy ...”

Rev. Dr. Martin Luther King, Jr.

at The Prayer Pilgrimage for Freedom, 1957

For those who wish to further explore the African American journey to freedom in America, including the fight for voting rights, there are two groundbreaking documentaries that may help us all to understand the racial disparities that have plagued our nation and governmental harmony for far too long. They are <u>MAAFA21. COM</u> and <u>ERRVIDEO.COM</u>

About MAAFA21 (The Documentary)

“They were stolen from their homes, locked in chains and taken across an ocean. And for more than 200 years, their blood and sweat would help to build the richest and most powerful nation the world has ever known. But WHEN SLAVERY ENDED, THEIR WELCOME WAS OVER.

America's wealthy elite had decided it was time for them to disappear and they were not particular about how it might be done. What you are about to see is that the plan these people set in motion 150 years ago is still being carried out today. So...

DON'T THINK THAT THIS IS HISTORY. IT IS NOT. IT IS HAPPENING RIGHT HERE, AND IT'S HAPPENING RIGHT NOW.”

About Emancipation Revelation Revolution
(ERR: The Documentary)

This is an award-winning documentary about the history of the civil rights movement in America; the role that both major political parties have played in it, and the voting habits of Blacks in America today.

As the nation is now divided — not only along racial lines — but along issues of morality and values — racial discrimination has been amped up by philosophical discrimination.

Why aren't Americans taught about the rich history of blacks in America, beyond the misperception of victimization?

Martin Luther King's dream has yet to be fully realized — with everyone in America being judged by the content of their character, not the color of their skin.

Again, human rights and privileges must not be determined and awarded based upon skin color. This is a season where we as human beings living in America need to be civil and nonviolent toward one another.

The word *civil* in Latin translates as "citizen," and is the root of the word "civilian." Therefore, civil civilian citizens resolve differences in a peaceful manner. The voting booth is a good place to start this process.

However, this principle of nonviolent civility applies not only to voting citizens in America. Even if you can't vote; for example, even if you have been a convicted felon and you're out of jail but haven't received a pardon, or your justice, or your opportunity to vote again; whoever you are, whether you vote or not, we are Americans. If we live in America and are citizens of America or even if we are not, we are citizens of planet earth, and God created all of us of one blood.

So, as we consider prison reform, anti-abortion legislation, anti-poverty legislation, health care legislation and so much more; we must remember that all votes matter, and the question of race should never hamper this process.

As an African American woman who is part African, part Irish, and part Native American, I know that all votes matter. All voices matter.

From my experience in America's political realm, and from the political perspective that I experienced when I ran for office in the 1970s and won, all the way up to my position as a State Legislator to the 28th House District of Georgia in the 1970s and 1980s, you can see that I'm old enough to have lived and voted in two centuries.

Yes, I was a Democrat at the time. And then I became an Independent. I also have been appointed to a commission, the Frederick Douglass Bicentennial Commission by President Donald John Trump. So, I hope this testimony lets you know that I'm not bound to party politics but that I tend to vote my convictions regardless of whichever party I'm working with at the time.

Of course, I stand for life as a civil right from conception or fertilization— from the womb to the tomb; for the sick; for the old; the elderly; for the rich and the poor; for no matter what ethnic group, or religion or skin color we are; for male and female.

The sanctity of life, not aborting babies, supporting mothers and fathers and babies and families all the way through life is very important.

As a female, I support women's rights. A woman has the right to choose what she does with her body but the baby is not her body. I still have to ask, "Where is the lawyer for the baby? How can the dream survive if we murder our children?"

I support the sanctity of marriage between a man and a woman as one of the strongest foundations that God has given us for success in life in the human family. I definitely support that.

I support the sanctity of religious freedom for everyone; not just for, and certainly not excluding, Christians.

I believe in taking care of the poor, the widows and orphans, and the least of these. However, there is a Scripture that says that if we don't work, we don't eat. So, regardless of skin color, social standing, or financial status; whether you are poor, middle class, working class, blue collar, or white collar, somewhere, somehow, someone should just consider that all of us, each and every one of us, can contribute to our society and make our society and our nation greater if we work, and we work together.

I believe that as Americans, regardless of skin color, or whether you are from different classes; the poor, the middle class, the working class, the blue collar, the white collar, the rich – we all have a part to play.

We are not asking for handouts, but a hand up. You know that policy that says if you teach a person to fish, they'll fish and eat for a lifetime, but if you give him a fish, they'll eat one meal for a day.

These are just examples of situations that I'm thinking and praying about. All votes matter.

I think that what I discovered having been a Democrat, an Independent, and a Republican is this: The Democrat platform offers deceptively "free entitlements" such as consequence-free "assistance" financed from government coffers all the while driving taxes to go higher and higher. The tax-subsidized "Office of Population Affairs" still exists in our government and needs to go.

On top of this, the Democrat Party has taken the African American vote for granted decades and decades. Their credo? Just keep playing the race card and promising them the world. We don't have to deliver. We already have their vote.

The Republican party is not blameless either. After decades of Black loyalty to the Democrat Party, the Republican Party has given up on the Black Vote and adopted this position: "We won't worry about the Black vote at all because they're going to vote for the Democrats anyway. Let's just do our thing."

However, it would behoove both parties along with the Independents to change their perspectives and realize that all votes matter.

Whether you're Latino, Hispanic, Caucasian, African American, Native American, Asian; if you're an American voter, wake up. Except for the Native Americans, we may have come into America on different boats, but we're all in the same boat now. Even for the immigrants who are coming in, if they go through a process that helps them to understand, know, and love America, and then become part of this beautiful country, they are welcome, too.

That should be the process. Immigrants should not expect to just storm into our country and say, "We're going to take everything you have and we want your country." No, that's not the way to do it. Please, we want to welcome our neighbors properly, with open arms; and begin to know, respect, love, and appreciate humanity together.

However, immigrants must know, respect and accept our mantra: "In God we trust." Without God, we are nothing. This way we can build some things together. Once we are citizens, we can vote for a greater nation.

So again, all votes matter. All voices matter. If you did not vote in the 2018 midterm elections, 2020 is upon us. Beyond that, as long as America exists, there are more elections ahead in the future.

Always, let's be civil, loving, non-violent, praying to God for a greater, stronger, better America, and a better world.

In 2016, I called for a moratorium on political strife in our family during the Thanksgiving and Christmas holidays. During that time, we broke bread, celebrated, and prayed together. We refused to contend about politics. We even went so far as to agree to go into the next year exercising our understanding and application of the six principles and the six steps of nonviolent conflict reconciliation that were a standard for the civil rights movement of the twenty-first century.

For me, these principles are more than just words on a page. They are treasured values that were taught and demonstrated by our elders. Now that I have become an elder in my generation, I still practice and model these proven methods with a measure of success that is being duplicated by the generations that follow me.

I apply these principles along with the Bible principles of repentance and forgiveness at work, in my community, and within my family. This is our circle of life.

SIX STEPS AND PRINCIPLES FOR NONVIOLENT SOCIAL CHANGE

A sequential journey to victory

Principle 1: Nonviolence is not passive, but requires courage.

Principle 2: Nonviolence seeks reconciliation, not defeat of an adversary.

Principle 3: Nonviolent action is directed at eliminating evil, not destroying an evildoer.

Principle 4: Is willing to accept suffering for the cause, if necessary, but never to inflict it.

Principle 5: Rejects hatred, animosity, and violence of the spirit, as well as refusing to commit physical violence.

Principle 6: Has faith that justice will prevail.

Understanding these principles, we apply the six steps of nonviolent conflict resolution.

1. Prayerfully enter into a process by conducting research and gathering information to get the facts straight.

2. Continuing in prayer, conduct education and awareness campaigns to inform adversaries and the public about the facts of the dispute.

3. Prayerfully commit yourself to live and manifest nonviolent attitudes and actions.

4. Prayerfully mediate and negotiate with the adversary in a spirit of goodwill to correct injustice.

5. Prayerfully apply nonviolent direct action, such as prayer vigils, marches, boycotts, mass demonstrations, picketing, sit-ins, etc., to help persuade or compel the adversary to work toward dispute-resolution.

6. Prayerfully anticipate reconciliation among adversaries in a win-win outcome that establishes a sense of community which should now be achievable.

[Available at:
http://www.civilrightsfortheunborn.org/non-violence.htm]

At the end of the day, reconciliation with our brothers and sisters should always be our goal. We must never allow politics to dampen our resolve in discovering and applying solutions to life's problems together. The manner in which we express respect, honor, love, and demonstrate equality to those from different cultural and ethnic backgrounds should never be dampened by ideological or political differences.

Reflection: How often do we find ourselves turning on news reports to see what is happening in the political arena before we even bow our heads in prayer to God? Why do we trust in human authority more than we trust in God?

—PRAYER—

Dear Heavenly Father, Your Word teaches us not to trust in horses and chariots, not in material power or human power, but to trust in You. Please help us to live Proverbs 3:5 more, which says, "Trust in the Lord with all of your heart." In Jesus's name, Amen.

Politics Can Make You

by Evangelist Alveda C. King

Politics can make you
Mad
Powerful
Excited
Politics can shape you, politics can break you
Politics can woo you —to spend and win
Politics can make you. God! Don't let it take you
Body
Soul
Spirit
Or politics can make you
A political animal

For the Lord does not see as man sees,
for man looks at the outward appearance,
but the Lord looks at the heart.
—1 Samuel 16:7 (NKJV)—

"THERE COMES A TIME WHEN ONE MUST TAKE
A POSITION THAT IS NEITHER SAFE NOR POLITIC
NOR POPULAR, BUT HE MUST TAKE IT BECAUSE
HIS CONSCIENCE TELLS HIM IT IS RIGHT."

—Dr. Martin Luther King, Jr.—

Ginger Speaks

Alveda and I went back and forth regarding how to talk about politics and its connection with racial tension in our book. In our country today, the political divisions and the racial divisions are probably the most heated and intense they have been in decades. Thus, we felt we had to address the elephant in the room and share our personal experiences with how race and politics have intersected in our own lives. Our hope is that, through sharing our perspectives on this topic, we are able to give our readers some insight as we all struggle to navigate our way through the current political environment.

Politics is likely the biggest hot button issue in our country today. The political climate is explosive, especially when racial issues are involved. I am very concerned that we have reached a dangerous place in our society when people are personally attacked because of their freedom of speech and their views and values. We demonize people and don't stop to listen to their point of view. This is concerning because we are Americans first before we are Democrats or Republicans, and we need to find common ground on that.

Given the heightened emotional nature of the political realm, it is tempting to make prejudiced assumptions about people on the opposite side of the aisle. Being prejudiced literally means prejudging a person or situation, having a "preconceived opinion that is not based on reason or actual experience."[1] It's so easy to label people based on their political affiliation, assuming that they have a certain mindset or perspective based on their party identity.

For example, some common misconceptions are that all Republicans are racists, and all Democrats don't care about the life of the unborn. These assumptions are obviously not true, but at times, we have all been affected by the negative rhetoric that suits our own party's narrative. Politics can divide us more than unite us, but my heart in writing this book is to focus on the things that can unite us. The important thing is we are all valuable as people, and we are all made in the image of a loving God who created us to be His image bearers.

As far as how race and politics collide, it is generally assumed in today's society (especially in the South) that most African Americans are Democrats and most Caucasians are Republicans, and this is problematic. People should have the freedom to align themselves with a particular party based on their personal *beliefs*, not based on the color of their skin. Much of the media fuels the racial political divide by sharing inflammatory and dramatic stories that stir up fear, hatred, and division. I have a personal experience with this that I'd like to share.

On January 15, 2018, I was privileged and honored to give a tribute to Dr. Martin Luther King Jr. It was his actual birthday and the fiftieth year of his passing. The commemorative service was held at the church where he and his father both pastored.

As I stepped up to the podium at Ebenezer Baptist Church that morning, I felt the hostility in the air. Standing underneath the projector screen with my name and title of "Georgia's Republican National Committeewoman," I could sense the friction. I sensed that just the word "Republican" by my name made people automatically assume things about who I was and what I believed. But, in that moment, the Holy Spirit directed me to say, "I come to you this morning in humility, asking you to judge me not by the color of my skin or the title that I hold, but as your sister in Christ who loves each and every one of you."

I literally felt the atmosphere in the room shift. It was a beautiful experience, one that I learned a great deal from. We have to realize that we can be on opposite political sides and still value and respect one another. I can love you, and you can love me, and we can be in two different parties and still have a relationship.

I believe, as our Vice President always says, that I am a Christian first, conservative second, and a Republican last. I am a Republican because I believe in the sanctity of life, personal responsibility, limited government, and lower taxes. However, I believe it's important to be able to agree to disagree with someone on the opposite side of the aisle in a respectful way.

One night, I went to La Parilla restaurant near my house for dinner. It was a Saturday night and very busy. I took a book called *My Life, My Love, My Legacy* by Coretta Scott King, which was given to me by her daughter, Bernice King[2]. I had to wait for a table, and there was an African American policeman who was on duty inside the restaurant. He noticed my book, asked me a question, and we struck up a conversation.

I told him that I was writing a book on racial reconciliation, and he gave me his approval saying that it needed to be done. He then shared some examples from his own life where he had been treated unfairly because of the color of his skin. He told me that he had moved from Gwinnett County to Atlanta because only white police officers were getting promoted in that area. I asked him how he thinks things can change, and he pointed to two young children and said, "Once people stop teaching children prejudice, that is when things will be different."

It really hit me between the eyes, because it is so true. We can teach our children to love, or we can teach them to hate. We have to choose to mirror love. Most of what children learn is caught, not taught.

Investing in the next generation has been a passion of mine for years. I have twin nephews who are my heart, and I pray they will never have prejudice toward anyone. I pray that they will love and treat all people as valuable and made in the image of God. I have taught and mentored young girls for over twenty years. I have led

Bible studies for young women in high school and through their post-graduate years, teaching hundreds of girls life lessons and values based on Biblical principles. I am still leading some of those same young women who are now in their late twenties and early thirties.

One of them, Emily Woods, has helped me in my political position, in speech writing, and in editing this book. She has a heart for racial reconciliation, and her thoughts were recorded in the Introduction to this book.

The purpose of this chapter is to encourage you to think for yourself rather than to rely on everything that you hear on the news or on what you may have previously assumed about race and politics. I urge you to stretch your perspective, to listen to people who disagree with you, and to seek understanding from people who have different life experiences that have shaped their political views. I believe that diversity in political parties is a needed and good thing, and my hope would be that Democrats and Republicans would challenge each other to have fresh eyes for the racial tensions that exist.

In our current political climate, the sad truth is that people can be so tied to their party's success that they throw everything else to the wayside. For example, many people are still so polarized by the 2016 election that they want to see our president fail more than they want to see racial reconciliation take place. My hope would be that we could see past all the racially charged propaganda that still exists in the media, and not let past assumptions pit us against each other. It has been a long and bruising two and a half years for our country, and my prayer is that we could see past the heated rhetoric and unify both racially and politically as the 2020 presidential election draws near.

I'll leave you with this thought that I shared at the Beloved Community Talks. Jesus was not a donkey or an elephant, He was the Lamb that was slain for the sins of the whole world. My heart is for us to look beyond party affiliations and treat each other with Christ-like sacrificial love and grace!

Reflection: In what way can you reach out to someone who is in a different political party than you? Is there someone you can invite to coffee, and honestly ask them why they support the party that they do? Can you just listen and not offer your opinion or belief system, then let them know you respect them and validate them as a person?

—PRAYER—

Dear Heavenly Father, help us to see each other as You see us. Help us not to focus on the outward appearance or outward sign of a party affiliation but instead to look at the heart of each person we come into contact with. Give us spiritual eyes to see others through the lens of kindness, compassion, and empathy. Enable us to bridge the divide, and to break down barriers and walls that have been built up from stereotypes that are both political and racial in nature. Help each of us to truly put politics aside and love each other with humility and grace. In Jesus's name, Amen.

While not everyone is a racist, it has always been easier for even the well intenders to turn a blind eye to strained race relations rather than rock the boat. In writing these chapters, Ginger and I are calling well-wishers out of the proverbial closet.

Chapter Four

DIFFERENT SIDES OF TOWN

For [Jesus] Himself is our peace,
who has made the two groups one
and has destroyed the barrier,
the dividing wall of hostility.

—Ephesians 2:14 (NIV)—

"PEOPLE FAIL TO GET ALONG BECAUSE THEY
FEAR EACH OTHER; THEY FEAR EACH OTHER
BECAUSE THEY DON'T KNOW EACH OTHER; THEY
DON'T KNOW EACH OTHER BECAUSE THEY HAVE
NOT COMMUNICATED WITH EACH OTHER."

—Dr. Martin Luther King Jr. —

Ginger Speaks

I spent all of my childhood in South Georgia. I was born in Waycross, and then my family moved to Thomasville when I was eighteen months old. During my early years, I frequently rode the train back to Waycross to visit my grandparents, who were two of the most influential people in my life. However, when I was twelve years of age, we ended up moving back to Waycross when my father died. My grandmother lived to be one hundred years old, but my grandfather passed away from colon cancer when he was only sixty-five years old.

My grandfather, affectionately known to his grandchildren as Dan Dan, was a public servant and a businessman. He served on the city council, becoming mayor in 1951, and later started several companies. He owned Herrin Brothers Furniture with his brother, founded Southern Bank, and used his success in business to bless others. One relevant example of his generosity is that he loaned money to an African American man to start his BBQ restaurant when no one else would at that time because of the racial biases.

On a recent visit to Waycross, my mother and I went to the Waycross courthouse to research city council meeting minutes from the years that my grandfather served. Even though Waycross was the segregated in the 1950s, I was thrilled to find that Dan Dan, in every instance, was a champion for the African American community. Though "colored only" signs indicated restrooms, water fountains, and back entrances for black people in their town, Dan Dan chose to treat every city member with dignity. He advocated for an athletic field and stop lights in black neighborhoods, and voted to grant a taxi license to an elderly African American cab driver.

HOUSE HELP

The following pages contain stories of my upbringing and family history. This was a very difficult chapter for me to write, because it has been painful for me to realize that my family participated in the racially segregated practices of the time.

My family was like other white families in Waycross that existed in segregated south and lived largely segregated lifestyles.

At that time, most African American women didn't have many other options for work besides being domestic helpers, and I am so thankful that our country has changed to give women of color other career opportunities! However, my family did have a number of African American women who were maids that worked for my mother's family, helping to raise her and taking care of my grandmother. In doing so, they helped make me into the woman I am today, and I am forever grateful for them. At the time, I didn't know any differently, but looking back, it's humbling and saddening to know that I naively was a part of the segregation. So, as you read these stories, know that I am bringing them to light with a heavy heart. My prayer is that my transparency would be healing and restorative in this conversation about race.

One night, I was mentally fatigued and decided to take a break from writing. After turning on the TV, I came across the movie *Hidden Figures*, and I felt a nudge from the Lord to watch the film.[1] It is based on a true story of three African American women who worked for NASA in 1961 and played important roles in helping astronaut John Glenn successfully travel to and from the moon. Although I had seen the movie twice before, God gave me new eyes to see the characters and the reality of the hardships an entire ethnic group of people faced during segregation.

There is a very moving scene in the film where the actress Taraji Henson (who plays Katherine Johnson) walks into the office entirely soaked from the rain. Her boss, Mr. Harrison, played by Kevin Costner, asked her where she had been for forty minutes.

She said, "There is no bathroom for me here."

He then replies, "What do you mean there is no bathroom for you here?"

She reiterates, "There is no bathroom. There are no colored bathrooms in this building, or any building outside the west campus, which is half a mile away. Did you know that? I have to walk to Timbuktu just to relieve myself."[2]

In the next scene, Mr. Harrison dramatically tears down the "colored only" restroom sign, and everyone is in the hall watching him. He then says, "No more colored restrooms, no more white restrooms. Here at NASA we all pee the same color."[3]

I was particularly touched by *Hidden Figures* because it gave me a better understanding of the cultural environment that my grandparents and parents lived in. As was the custom in the South, my grandmother always had a maid helping her around the home. When my mom and her siblings were growing up, a very special maid named Ellen took care of them for nearly twenty-five years.

One Christmas, I asked Nana how Ellen came to work for them. These were her words: "Well, your mother was sick, so Dan Dan got in the car and drove over to Colored Town, and he saw a woman sitting on her front porch. He got out of the car, and said, 'Excuse me, ma'am, do you know of anyone who could help my wife take care of our sick baby?' And Ellen replied, 'Let me go get my apron.'"

And the rest is history! Ellen worked for my family for the rest of her life. My grandparents and their children adored Ellen, and the love was mutual. Ellen named her grandsons after my grandfather and his best friend, which meant the world to my family. I never got to meet Ellen, but I've heard so much about her that I can't wait to meet her in heaven!

When I was a little girl, my grandparents had a maid named Bertha. After my father passed away, we moved back to Waycross and lived with Nana for a few months. My grandfather died when I was in the fourth grade. I remember Bertha as a funny but tough woman who didn't put up with any monkey business from my brothers or myself; and, she made the best fried chicken! When she died, our family attended her funeral and were the only white people in the church. It was an amazing service celebrating Bertha's homegoing.

After Bertha died, her daughter Yvonne came to work for my grandmother, and she was with Nana until the day she died at one hundred years old. Nana loved Yvonne, and Yvonne loved Nana. Toward the end of her life, I spent several weeks with Nana, and some days I would walk in her room and Yvonne would just be sitting there holding Nana's hand.

I remember reading the book *The Help* one summer, and I took it to Nana's but didn't bring it out when Yvonne was around, in case it made her feel uncomfortable.[4] I wondered if she ever felt like the women depicted in Kathryn Stockett's book based on African-American women working in Caucasian households in Jackson, Mississippi, during the early 1960s. Growing up in South Georgia, most of my friends' parents had maids, as was typical during that time period. My family did not have steady house-help, but I do remember one maid going to the beach with us to take care of my youngest brother after he was born.

I hated to think that Yvonne ever felt discriminated against or unappreciated like the maids in *The Help*, though there are many things in the book that were true in my own family. For example, there was an old bathroom in my grandparents' carport that was set aside for their house-help to use. Additionally, my grandfather built a beach cottage that had a tiny room in the garage, and my siblings and I discovered the room when we were playing hide-and-seek. Confused about what it was used for, I asked my mom. She pointed out an old cot in the corner and told me that the tiny room used to be where Ellen slept when she would come to the beach with them.

It is surreal for me to think that even in my own family, people who worked for them had to use a different bathroom and sleep in a garage because of the color of their skin. Furthermore, my early paternal ancestors owned slaves, which is a part of my family history that grieves me deeply. I am so thankful that our laws have changed, but unfortunately, in many places in the South, certain prejudices still remain.

That is one of the reasons Alveda and I wanted to write this book. Knowing our history is important and trying to understand all of it—the good, the bad, and the ugly—is necessary. If we don't learn from our past, then we will repeat it.

FRIENDSHIP

Growing up, all of my closest friends were white. There were two African American girls on my cheerleading squad, and we had a cordial relationship, but they never came to my house, and I never went to theirs. Waycross was still segregated in many ways. My first real friendship with an African American woman was forged when I moved to Atlanta and started attending Church of the Apostles. A few rows in front of me, I noticed a beautiful African American woman who wore authentic African clothes and could pray like nobody's business. I would look up and see her week after week. One day the Holy Spirit prompted me to ask her to pray for me. She did, and Ida Mitchell and I have been prayer partners ever since.

Ida has mentored me and taught me so much these last twenty years. She hears from God and has so many amazing gifts she has imparted to me. I remember one day about ten years ago, one of my Bible study girls called me after church. She had observed Ida and I worshipping together at the service. She said that, as she watched Ida and I sing together, she had this sense that heaven will look similar; very different people standing together to praise the same God. And I agree that heaven will have people from every tribe and nation worshiping together without an ounce of segregation or prejudice. But it is so sad that here on Earth eleven o'clock on Sunday morning may be the most segregated hour of the week.

In 2001, soon after I opened my store, I made a very unlikely friendship with an older black man named Henry. At the time, Henry was homeless and used to come into my shop and ask me for money. He always reeked of liquor, and I eventually learned that he was an alcoholic. When he'd stop by my shop, we would walk down the shopping strip together to the White House restaurant and have lunch. I also would give him a little money every now and then.

One day after giving him some cash, I told him that I wouldn't be giving him any more money because I did not want him spending it on alcohol. He later told this story to my Sunday School class and said, "I got to the beer store and had the six pack in my hands, but as I was going to pay for it, I remembered Ginger's face and the love of God in her eyes. I couldn't buy the beer." He then went on to say that he was immediately delivered from alcoholism and never drank again. It was a miracle.

I continued to be friends with Henry, helping him secure a job and get off the streets. Amazingly, he started helping rescue others from homelessness as well. I share this story to say that though Henry and I were an unlikely pair, God brought us together, and we formed a very special friendship. Not only was he a dear friend, but he ended up saving my life.

Every December, I helped deliver Christmas presents to children who had a parent in prison through a ministry called Angel Tree. I usually brought my Bible study girls with me, but this particular year, they were all unable to come, so Katherine, a sixteen-year-old who worked at my store, offered to accompany me instead. I mentioned our plans to Henry, and he insisted that he come with us to downtown Atlanta to help deliver the presents.

The day went smoothly until our final delivery. We pulled up to a rundown apartment complex with bars on the windows, and I stepped out of my Volvo, dressed to the nines and feeling very out of place. Two young teenagers seemed to be standing guard, watching us closely as we approached. I knocked on the apartment door and someone yelled, "Who's there?"

I replied in my squeaky high-pitched voice, "We're delivering presents for Angel Tree," and I mentioned the child's name.

The door opened abruptly, and a half-dressed woman stood before us. To make a long story short, we walked in on a drug deal. I think God protected us by letting me look totally stupid. I even asked if they would let Henry pray for them.

When we got back in the car, Henry explained everything that was happening, and we all truly believe that if Henry had not been with us, we would have been killed. It was such a dangerous situation that our church stopped participating in Angel Tree after that. Henry, Katherine, and I told the story to our Sunday School and there was a former Georgia Bureau Investigation officer in the class. He said that he wouldn't have gone into the neighborhood where we went alone, even wearing a bulletproof vest. God protected us for sure, and he used Henry to do it!

I share these stories to demonstrate Jesus' transformative power in my life, as He has totally renewed my own view and understanding of race over the years. Although I am a southern white woman who comes from a family that owned slaves and later employed black maids, I truly am not colorblind as to the upbringing I had, and I now intentionally seek out friendships with people who are racially different from me. Alveda, Ida, and Henry are just a few of my close friends who are African American, and they have so much insight into things that I don't.

For example, Henry humbled me with his kindness, his work ethic, and his resilience in the face of all the trials he endured. His gratitude for every little thing in his life challenged me to intentionally choose to be thankful for even the small things in my own life. My friend Ida has been an invaluable rock and source of wisdom to me over the years and has helped me understand the racial divide as well. When I shared with her my experience of visiting an all-black church and that many in the congregation were not kind to me, she replied to me, "Now you know how we feel." I have since been more aware of how marginalized African Americans can feel in all white settings or congregations.

And lastly, Alveda has helped me truly understand what it means to not be colorblind and at times has called and been very frank with me in asking me hard questions. That is the meaning of a true friend. Her friendship is invaluable to me.

Reflection: Is there someone you know who has a different skin color than you have? What can you do to forge a friendship with that person? Ask God to show you someone and commit to reaching out to them this week. Don't delay. You could have a brand-new friendship and learn a great deal from them.

—PRAYER—

Dear Heavenly Father, we come to You humbly asking that You help us see each other through Your loving eyes. Help us to take time to reflect on our own stories and to repent of any ways that we have acted with prejudice toward others. Lord, help us to take the beam out of our own eye before we try to take the speck out of someone else's. Racism is a terrible sin that has divided our nation for far too long. We repent and ask You to help us see the values we share more than the things that cause us to live in hostility toward one another. Show us how to truly forgive and receive forgiveness. In Jesus's name, Amen.

Alveda Speaks

When I was a young girl during the Christmas holidays in both Atlanta and later in Birmingham and Louisville, my dad would drive our family around into the various communities to see the Christmas decorations. The really big homes with myriads of lights were on the "white" side of town. The mansions were, of course, spectacular.

I learned early that, while we lived in nice neighborhoods, there were different parts of town where different ethnic communities were populated. For instance, in Atlanta, we lived near downtown. Uptown was where the "swells" or primarily the prominent and wealthy Caucasian communities were.

There were varying sections called the "poor" side of town where in some areas Caucasians lived, and other areas Negroes (as we were called back then) lived. Interestingly, my mother Naomi came from a different side of town than my daddy did. It didn't matter to Daddy though. He was determined to make his "little girl," as he called her, his bride. And he did.

Before I ramble on and change the direction of this chapter, let me explain that it isn't uncommon for people of like ethnicities and economic achievements to want to live in neighborhoods with people who share the same status. This sentiment in and of itself is not racism. Racism occurs in situations where communal polarization is based upon skin color. Throughout the twentieth century, racial profiling in real estate, and other shameful forms of racism were very prevalent. Ginger and I are both products of our times—times which we are attempting to illustrate with the hopes of resolution and reconciliation for our readers. Redlining is a discriminatory practice in which certain neighborhoods are targeted for exclusion to services or financial support. The most common example of redlining occurs when a bank or insurance company denies service to residents of financially distressed communities that have a high non-white population. I experienced redlining firsthand in the Fair Housing Movement of the 1960s when protestors fought against selective bargaining in housing debates.

One thing that both Ginger and I have observed is that while not everyone is a racist, it has always been easier for even the well intenders to turn a blind eye to strained race relations rather than rock the boat. Many people have never agreed to the practice of sustaining segregated communities, but because of peer pressure, they have remained silent on the issues. In writing these chapters, Ginger and I are calling well-wishers out of the proverbial closet.

This, of course, doesn't mean that we can't be selective in designing our own spaces. It means that we must work hard at avoiding discrimination in the process.

Having said this, we can acknowledge that certain parts of town can just have a certain "feel" about them. For instance, artists like to gather in spaces and places that are relaxed and sometimes almost bohemian in nature. Some communities attract families who enjoy perfectly manicured lawns. Some people like to live in areas with townhouses and lofts. All of these settings represent freedom of expression.

Just as every family and even every tribe has one or more God-ordained talents or skill sets the same can be said for certain communities. For example, in the Bible, the twelve tribes of Israel had varying natural and spiritual assignments. The Levites were the priestly branch. Issachar understood the signs of the times. Sons of Zebulon were seafaring communities.

It would follow that people will gather and live near friends and family who fit in with their lifestyles to a certain degree. Yet, when those decisions are shaped around skin color and ethnicity, the specter of racism begins to rear its beady head.

Having been born into the Williams-King tribe, a family that historically and generationally has been called to serve humanity, I have enjoyed the experience of accepting people as children of God. As a guardian of the King Family Legacy in my generation, I am often called to teach repentance, forgiveness, and love to the nations of the world. Understanding this, I urge people to see each other as units of the overall human family. Our bloodlines and blood ties are important, but they should not divide us.

The human experience has many facets and frequencies which cause people to be born into certain conditions, and yes, even certain communities. Yet, at the end of the day, as you will read over and over again in this book, we are all one-blood, one-race human beings. We should never seek to divide ourselves from each other for reasons such as skin color, economic privilege or lack of such, or all of the other human conditions that people tend to fight about. I will dare to say that we should not even fight over religious preferences.

Ginger and I have talked about being born into diverse communities. When I was a young girl, I'd hear people say things like, "She was born on the wrong side of town." Or you'd hear a phrase like "the poor side of town" or "the colored neighborhood." Then too, they would refer to the part of town I grew up in as the "west side," which pretty much also meant the colored side of town. Some of these distinctions were due to skin color, and some due to socioeconomic conditions. For example, the term "poor white trash" wasn't referring to black people or Negroes as we were called in those days.

Uncle ML once wrote, "Property is intended to serve life, and no matter how much we surround it with rights and respect, it has no personal being. It is part of the earth man walks on. It is not man."[6]

At the end of the day, we as human beings have more in common than we have differences. As President Trump said in his inaugural speech, "We all bleed the same." So, it doesn't matter so much what street we live on, what town we come from, what our pedigrees are. We can't let our differences become wedges.

Reflection: Have our pedigrees become a source of pride and arrogance in our lives?

—PRAYER—

Dear Heavenly Father, teach me to love my neighbor as myself and to reach beyond politics to realize and recognize every person as a human being, created by God, in Jesus's name, Amen.

Chapter Five

SHARED FAMILY VALUES

———◉———

God places the lonely in families;
He sets the prisoners free and gives them joy.
But He makes the rebellious live
in a sun-scorched land.

—Psalm 68:6—

———◉———

Alveda Speaks

Somehow in the late twentieth century America, the concept of living according to Biblical principles became relegated to a political viewpoint. In other words, if a person believed and supported living according to the principles laid out in the Bible, they were supporting a new byword called "family-values" and connecting themselves to conservative viewpoints and a conservative political platform.

Along the way, "family values" were demonized to such a point that certain political factions in America wanted those values labeled as "hate crimes." I outline this historical occurrence to point out that life wasn't always that way in America.

As Ginger and I have pointed out in our previous chapters, we grew up in diverse neighborhoods where we experienced upbringings that were similar in some ways and different in others. Through the years of our friendship, Ginger and I have discovered that we share much in common. Our shared concept of what matters in life includes appreciation of what some still call "family values."

While Ginger and I were both brought up in Christian homes, there were differences, of course. Yet, the core of our upbringing and the remaining basis of our faith is established in Jesus Christ. We both attend church regularly, and we both adhere to Biblical principles as much as we are able.

While our life experiences may appear to be very different on the surface, Ginger and I have shared life experiences as well as family values. Both of our fathers died under tragic circumstances at early ages. My dad was killed in the crosshairs of the civil rights movement. Ginger's father battled with depression and a resulting medication overdose. Both of our fathers struggled with the demon of alcohol consumption. So, Ginger and I grew up under a cloud of grief to some extent.

However, with both of our families being grounded in the Judeo-Christian faith, Ginger and I also continue to share an abiding faith that overcomes the tragedies of the world. It is this faith, which works by agape love, to unite me with Ginger across and far beyond any barriers.

Having grown up in a family that is firmly established in the principles of faith and agape love, I am also grateful to be attached as a member of Believers' Bible Christian Church (BBCC) in Atlanta, Georgia. I've been at BBCC for over thirty years where I was blessed to have Pastor Allen McNair as my mentor. When Pastor McNair left earth for heaven in 2015, his son Pastor Theo Jr. stepped into the role of leader of the ministry. Thankfully, there has been no break in the spiritual stability that adds to my life and ministry even today.

While writing this book, I have attended church services at BBCC with the great and blessed expectation of receiving wisdom and knowledge that is shared with you in this book. It is a valued treasure to have a storehouse of wisdom and truth garnered not only from my forefathers in the King Family Legacy, but to also have more of the same at my home church.

One particular message from Pastor Teddy resonates in the same frequency as this chapter. I remember attending service one Sunday with a heavy heart. I whispered a prayer before taking my position on the platform with our worship team. My soul was very burdened with the cares of the world that were reflected from having to attend social and family gatherings and have people around me criticize me for my association and friendship with President Donald Trump.

By then, things had escalated to such a point that people were recognizing my face and stopping me in shopping mall parking lots, or in the airport and other public places, to berate me for having voted for the president. Even church wasn't safe anymore, as many of our members were outraged with me for my support of President Trump. I was dreading going around familiar places.

After the worship team finished our last song, and we went to our seats, Pastor Theo began teaching a very timely message. He talked about relationships that day and how important it is to take opportunities to "spend time with those who share your values." While Pastor Teddy encouraged us to love everyone and to approach everyone with Christian love, he also said that it is important to spend time with people who agree with us, as well as affirm our values.

This principle, working and living with those who share our values, is so important. This is the case with Ginger and me. We are not separated by skin color or socioeconomic conditions; we are united by faith and love, as well as Christian and family values.

Reflection: Is it possible to enjoy the company of those who share our values without harming important relationships with our families, in the workplace and other social settings, as well as in our church experiences?

—PRAYER—

Dear Heavenly Father, help us to value Your Word in our everyday lives; in our worship, which is our relationship with You; and in our relationships with those around us. Help us to embrace those values in our family legacies that add to our lives, and to release those values that do not align themselves with Your Word, in Jesus's Name, Amen.

> *"I HAVE A DREAM THAT MY FOUR LITTLE*
> *CHILDREN WILL ONE DAY LIVE IN A NATION*
> *WHERE THEY WILL NOT BE JUDGED BY THE*
> *COLOR OF THEIR SKIN, BUT BY THE CONTENT*
> *OF THEIR CHARACTER."*
>
> —Dr. Martin Luther King Jr. —

How great is the love the Father has lavished on us
that we should be called children of God!
And that is what we are!

—1 John 3:1 (NIV)—

Ginger Speaks

In the previous chapter, Alveda and I shared about our different upbringings. Every time I reflect on those differences and the fact that the Lord has brought us together, I'm overwhelmed with gratitude and awe that God has unified us in mind, heart, and soul through writing this book. If Alveda and I had nothing else in common other than the fact we share the same heavenly Father, that would be all we would need to have shared family values. The truth is that, although our paths have been different, we come from contrasting cultures, and we were raised in different times, we still share a bond that is deeper than any difference we have; we share our love for the Lord Jesus.

Interestingly, Alveda and I have had some similar life experiences. We both lost our fathers in sudden and tragic ways early in life, and we still carry wounds from their deaths. We both grew up in the church, but we had to make our faith our own by personally committing our lives to Jesus Christ. The King family name is synonymous with Baptist preachers, nonviolence, and civil rights. Theirs is a legacy of love and sacrifice. My family on my mother's side was very civic-minded. As I mentioned earlier, my grandfather was the mayor of Waycross, serving on the city commission and starting several businesses. Although my father was only thirty-seven years old when he died, he too gave back to our community in Thomasville by serving on several boards and committees.

Alveda and I both agree that ultimately, the best legacy a family can leave the next generation is one of living out unconditional love. And no one showed us the true meaning of unconditional love like Jesus. He is our ultimate role model, and if we want to share in His values, then we need to watch Him in action and how He treated people of different ethnicities. Jesus never discriminated against anyone. Let's look at a passage from Scripture where Jesus interacts with a Samaritan woman at a well. In Biblical times, a Jewish man like Jesus was expected to hate Samaritans, but instead, He respectfully addressed the woman and asked her to give Him a drink of water.

"Then the woman of Samaria said to Him, 'How is it that You, being a Jew, ask a drink from me, a Samaritan woman? For Jews have no dealings with Samaritans.' Jesus answered and said to her, 'If you knew the gift of God, and who it is who says to you, "give Me a drink," you would have asked Him, and He would have given you living water. Jesus answered and said to her, "Whoever drinks of this water will thirst again, but whoever drinks of the water that I shall give him will never thirst. But the water that I shall give him will become in him a fountain of water springing up into everlasting life" (John 4:9–10, 13–14 NKJV).

First of all, men in Biblical times usually did not speak to women in public. Furthermore, the fact that the woman was a Samaritan and Jesus was a Jew made it all the more interesting because Jews typically despised Samaritans. In the same way that Jesus broke from societal stereotypes and norms, we need to step outside of the natural tendency to prejudge people and engage with them as equal and valuable human beings. We have the opportunity to pursue and embrace people who are different than us, just as Jesus did at the well.

The story ends beautifully as the Samaritan woman recognizes Jesus as the Messiah and goes to tell others in the town about Him. It is a marvelous example of how to love others who may be different than we are. God tells us the first commandment is to love Him with all our heart, mind, and soul, and the second is to love our neighbor as ourselves. (See Matthew 22:36–40.)

Wow, stop and think about that for a minute. Who is your neighbor? Who is my neighbor? Is it the homeless man we passed by on the street today? Is it the old woman at church who has no family? Is it the young man in prison?

As children of God, may the Lord help us realize that our shared heavenly value of love sees beyond ethnicity, politics, socio-economic barriers, religion, and so many other things.

Reflection: How can you today reach out to someone who is entirely different from you? Is there someone whom you have a prejudice about? What can you do to see them through a different lens as Jesus did with the woman at the well?

—PRAYER—

Dear Heavenly Father, help us to recognize that the most important value we have together is a love for Jesus, which manifests in a love for other people. Give us a fresh perspective that every opportunity to interact with others is a chance to show Your love and kindness, pointing them to the true living water of Jesus Christ. Give us boldness to move beyond hatred and judgment of those who are different from us and to recognize that every human being is in need of unconditional love and acceptance. In Jesus's name, Amen.

GINGER'S PHOTO GALLERY

Ginger's family– Mom, Dad, David, Scott & me

Ginger with both of her great grandmothers

Ginger's grandmother's 90th birthday. She lived to be 100.

American Beach Story

Historic African American beach. This is the beach African Americans were allowed to go to.

Picture of MLK in the home of the woman who helped Ginger's grandmother.

My Grandfather Dan Dan, who was the Mayor of Waycross & a great advocate for the Black community

Ginger & Alveda

Ginger with Bernice,
Dr. Martin Luther King's daughter

Picture from MLK Day

Ginger with her nephews, Robert and Will

110

ALVEDA'S PHOTO GALLERY

Alveda's dad & uncle

MLK with Billy Graham

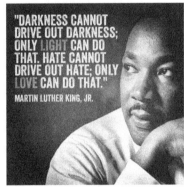

"DARKNESS CANNOT DRIVE OUT DARKNESS; ONLY LIGHT CAN DO THAT. HATE CANNOT DRIVE OUT HATE; ONLY LOVE CAN DO THAT."

MARTIN LUTHER KING, JR.

Rev. A.D. King, Rev. Fred Shuttlesworth and Rev. Andrew Young leading prayer at a peaceful protest

King Family

King Family Multi Generations

King Family

AD, father and MLK

Wedding of Aaron King and Angela Stanton King;
Evangelist Alveda King, Officiant

113

Black History Month at the White House in 2020

President Trump signs MLK Park executive order

Evangelist Alveda King prays at rally.

Angela, Trevian, Ginger, Sharon and Alveda with Mike Lindell

As a Christian Evangelist I am for humanity. As such, I believe we are not separate races; we are one blood, one human race. Racial division is a socially engineered, divisive concept.
I am for human rights, and human dignity; for everyone, from the womb to the tomb. I support the US Constitution and the clear connection to a biblical world view therein.

WWW.CIVILRIGHTSFORTHEUNBORN.ORG

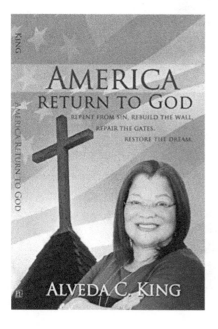

Chapter Six

BELOVED COMMUNITY TALKS

---◉---

Beloved, let us love one another,
for love is of God; and everyone who loves
is born of God and knows God.

—1 John 4:7—

---◉---

"LOVE IS THE ONLY FORCE CAPABLE OF
TRANSFORMING AN ENEMY INTO A FRIEND."

—Dr. Martin Luther King Jr. —

"WE MUST DEVELOP AND MAINTAIN THE CAPACITY
TO FORGIVE. HE WHO IS DEVOID OF THE POWER TO
FORGIVE IS DEVOID OF THE POWER TO LOVE. THERE
IS SOME GOOD IN THE WORST OF US AND SOME EVIL IN
THE BEST OF US. WHEN WE DISCOVER THIS, WE ARE
LESS PRONE TO HATE OUR ENEMIES."

—Dr. Martin Luther King Jr. —

Ginger Speaks

In August of 2017, I was asked to participate in a discussion at the Martin Luther King Jr. Center entitled "Beloved Community Talks: Let's Bridge the Racial Divide." Dr. Bernice King, daughter of Dr. King and CEO of The King Center, and Dr. Kendra King Momon, professor of politics at Oglethorpe University, were the moderators. In honor of Coretta Scott King, the founder of the Beloved Community, the theme of the talk that evening was "Women...the Soul of a Nation," which focused on the unique role of women in racial reconciliation. It was also to commemorate the fifty-fourth anniversary of the "I Have a Dream" speech.

The women conversationalists were as follows: Senator Elizabeth Warren, social activist Tamika Mallory, clinical psychologist Dr. Gloria Morrow, CNN political contributor Margaret Hoover, faith leader and FOX News contributor Alveda King, and me as Republican National Committeewoman for Georgia.

At the time of our meeting, the wounds were still very fresh from the violence and hatred in Charlottesville, Virginia, and you could feel the high tension in the room and friction in the air. The event was held at Ebenezer Baptist Church. There was a big crowd, and I sat next to Alveda on the stage.

When we took our seats, the moderators started asking questions and soon the fireworks began. I don't remember exactly how it happened, but there were much hatred and venom spewed toward Alveda because of her support for President Trump. It was very difficult to sit there and watch my friend being personally attacked because of who she voted for in an election, but she handled it with grace and love.

I was the last person to be asked a question, and I was beginning to think they weren't going to address me. And honestly, at that point, I would have been glad to stay silent. However, Bernice King finally asked me a question along the lines of how I could help heal the racial divide as a conservative.

I wish I could tell you word-for-word what I said, but even my notes that I had practiced didn't help me to voice my heart on that question. I had seen real pain and hurt from some of the panelists and many in the audience, and I was overwhelmed by the gravity of the emotions.

I started off by acknowledging that I have had a different life experience, and I did not know what it was like to grow up being discriminated against because of the color of my skin. However, I deeply wanted to listen and to understand. I said that Jesus is our greatest example of reconciliation, and He has given us the ministry of reconciliation. I also said that Jesus was not a donkey or an elephant, but He was the Lamb that was slain for the sins of the whole world. I shared how God made us all in His image to be His image-bearers, and we were made from one God who loves each and every one of us. Our differences should be celebrated, and God made many different ethnicities, nations, and people groups, but we can embrace our differences and try and put ourselves in each other's shoes.

I think it is important to show up to events like this one. It would have been easier and more comfortable for me to politely decline the invitation, avoiding a difficult discussion on a heated topic. Instead, it was one of the best decisions I have ever made. I am sorry to admit that it took me such a long time to realize this, but that night showed me loud and clear that there is still a deep wound in our country's racial divide.

Had I not taken part in the panel, I may still have been going about my life with a la-dee-da attitude that everything is just peachy. It is not just peachy. Many people have some very deep scars that cannot be healed after one panel discussion on healing the racial divide. It took us a long time to get here, and it will take a long time to heal, but I want to see this in my lifetime. The Lord burdened my heart to be a bridge builder through showing the love of Jesus, and writing this book was the first step in carrying out that calling.

Until I watched the Royal Wedding of Prince Harry and Meghan Markle, I did not know that Meghan is ethnically blended. Her mother is African American, and her father is Caucasian. Fifty years ago, it would have been a total impossibility for a prince to marry someone that not only did not have royal blood but was of a mixed race. It warmed my heart to see the African American bishop, Michael Curry, give an uplifting and charismatic sermon at the wedding. Here is a quote from his text citing Dr. King, "Dr. Martin Luther King Jr. once said, 'We must discover the power of love, the redemptive power of love. And when we discover that, we will be able to make of this old world a new world. Love is the only way.'"[1]

What a wonderful truth! I was so inspired by his sermon and by the fact that Dr. King's dream lives on. I can only imagine the rejoicing in heaven when he looked down to see the great-great-great-granddaughter of a slave, sitting in Windsor Castle, watching her daughter marry a real live prince. It's even better than a fairytale ending.

The greatest power in the world is love, and the true source of love is God. The Bible says in 1 John 4:8, "Whoever does not love does not know God, because God is love" (NIV). And 1 John 3:16 shows us the definition of true love: "By this we know love, because He laid down His life for us. And we also ought to lay down our lives for the brethren" (NIV).

I had a prophetic dream about this book while sleeping in my bed one night. Alveda's uncle Martin had a dream in the form of an ideal vision of God's colorful creation coming together in love and unity, bearing His glorious image. Both of those dreams are being realized through this book.

I know that it's God's heart for injustice to be righted. Ultimately, if our hearts are in the right place, He can use us. I believe that this book is appropriately timed because we want to finish what Dr. King and many others started. We've made great strides, but we still have a long way to go. Laws don't change hearts; only God changes hearts. I pray God will change hearts one at a time. As Jesus says in John 10:35, "By this everyone will know that you are my disciples, if you love one another." (NIV)

Reflection: Have you ever felt the heaviness of the wounds of racial division in our country in a conversation with others? If so, what would it look like to meditate on what you felt and asked God to show you how to be a part of healing?

—PRAYER—

Dear Heavenly Father, You call us beloved, which means dearly loved. You showed us what true love is by sending Your one and only Son to die as our substitute. You gave us His perfect love and taught us how to love by showing us real love. You have also given us Your Word as a guide to study and learn how to love like You do. Forgive us, Lord. We have failed You and failed others miserably. Help us to heal the hurts and the wounds that we have inflicted upon each other. Give us Your grace and mercy to extend to our brothers and sisters in a way that will revolutionize our society. In Jesus's name, Amen.

Alveda Speaks

In dissecting the word *beloved*, we can see that a command is issued in the term— "Be love." In dissecting the word *beloved* we see both a command and an invitation to love and *be* loved. God is love. We are created in God's image, so we radiate and are reflections of His love. This is not an erotic or emotional love, but an all-encompassing love that has the power to heal brokenness and bridge divisions. Because we are loved by God, we can love and be loved by others.

As I join Ginger in writing this chapter, I realize that she and I are obeying this commandment as we work together to answer the call of God to be salt and light in our generation.

Prior to the "Beloved Community Talks" series founded by my cousin the Reverend Dr. Bernice King, chairman of the Martin Luther King Jr. Center for Nonviolent Social Change and "Be a King" Ministries, Ginger and I traveled in the same political conservative circles and also were united in Christ by our faith. However, we discovered the close friendship bond after the heated and controversial session of the talks which occurred at the historical site of Ebenezer Baptist Church in Atlanta during the summer of 2017.

As Ginger describes, in one of the sessions, we were part of a platform of women who, to put it mildly, had opposing viewpoints on issues of the day. Senator Elizabeth Warren had preceded us in a one-on-one discussion with Reverend Bernice. Ginger and I were part of the next session, in a panel setting. I'm not sure that any of us on the panel were prepared for the angst, vitriol, and pain that were unwrapped in that sixty-minute diatribe. However, as things proceeded, I realized that this was a beautiful *kairos* moment for me where I could enact the six principles and six steps of nonviolent conflict reconciliation that I listed in chapter 3.

In the heat of the panel discussion, where the record of President Trump was being ferociously examined, my position of support for the President came under fire. When my opportunity to respond to the challenge was delayed, I mentally reviewed my commitment to my cousin Reverend Bernice to not only participate in the discussion but also do my best to be fair and objective.

I remember scrunching down in my seat under the verbiage that was being directed toward me. Finally, it was time for me to speak, and as I recall, I said something like this: "Love never fails. I love you right now."

Then everything went silent. You could hear the proverbial pin drop as the air seemed sucked out of the room in those precious seconds. Every angry retort was staunched, at least for a moment.

Then, the moderator said something like this, "We may not agree with Auntie [that's me], but we can agree to be civil."

I must admit to you that in that hour, I wanted to flee the stage. We were running overtime and I did have another engagement to attend for the rest of the evening. However, I stayed and toughed it out.

Ginger was there on stage. Her remarks, while brief, had received a more favorable reception than my presence in the room had elicited so far. I wonder if the color of her skin and the color of mine had anything to do with all of it? Believe me, I wasn't colorblind in any of those moments. I saw Ginger's fair skin and all the differing hues of all of the women there. However, I knew we were in way deep, way beyond the skin-color battles. Our mutually redeeming factor was that Ginger and I were following God's pattern of repentance, forgiveness, and love. We didn't lay the blame on our attackers. We took the blame and bore the shame and depended on love to win the day. And agape love won. God's love always wins.

The verbal attacks that I experienced that night came from one of the black panelists, so ideology was the issue rather than skin color. I was able to stand in love while standing my ground amid the tirade by taking a deep breath and silently quoting John 3:16

to myself, "For God so loved …" I reflected on how God loved me, this panelist, and the whole world. I also mentally reviewed the Six Steps of Nonviolent Conflict Resolution. So, when the time came for me to speak, the first words out of my mouth were, "I love you."

A note on verbiage:

At the beginning of the chapter, as Ginger discusses her perception of the Beloved Community Talks and her reaction to the wedding of Prince Harry and Meghan Markle, Ginger uses phrases such as biracial and multiracial. Ginger and I have talked about these phrases to describe race, and this is one of those perceptional points where we communicate differently. For me, there is no biracial or multiracial person to consider, because there are not separate races of human beings. Only one blood and one race.

Sometimes, when Ginger and I talk and she will use one of the familiar terms, I'll say something like, "I hear you, Ginger, but there's only one race so they can't be biracial or anything like that." She'll laugh and say something like, "I see what you mean! For me though, these terms are culturally relevant and helpful to use in certain contexts." We are learning from each other's perspectives, and we find it so helpful to talk through different cultural verbiage surrounding race to better understand one another.

I was out with some friends recently, and the same thing happened. I stopped the conversation in mid-sentence and quoted Acts 17:26. This is a hard idea to learn and accept, let alone live in that reality. We are working on it.

126

Reflection: Is there hope for a "beloved community?"

—PRAYER—

Dear Heavenly Father, please help us to learn to repent, forgive, and love each other as we seek Your heavenly guidance for finding that "beloved community" in our hearts. In Jesus's name, Amen.

One person can make a difference, just like Dr.
Martin Luther King, Jr. His decision to stand up
for righteousness and truth changed the course of
history. We now have that same choice.
Will you ... be a bold voice of healing and unity
to bridge the racial divide?

KING WEEK 2018

---◉---

But let justice run down like water, and
righteousness like a mighty stream.

— Amos 5:24 (NKJV)—

---◉---

Ginger Speaks

I was humbled and honored to be invited back to Ebenezer Baptist Church to give a tribute to Dr. Martin Luther King, Jr. on the fiftieth anniversary of the annual commemoration service of his life. I was told I had only three minutes to deliver my speech, and that I had to stay on time because the event was being televised. However, right before I went on, they told me that I actually had five minutes to speak. Though I had only prepared for three minutes, God gave me the extra time to share what was on His heart for the people that day.

Some of the speeches before mine were very divisive and not in the spirit of Dr. King. I can only imagine how it would have grieved him to know that instead of standing up for righteousness and truth, many on the platform were using their time as an opportunity for partisan politics. Several people in the audience had walked with Dr. King and been in the civil rights movement with him, and I could sense their wounds from years of division. I could sympathize with them but could not relate to their emotions. Dr. Ben Carson was one of the speakers, and even he was not received warmly.

When it was my turn to speak, I felt the Holy Spirit direct me to change my opening and that is when I said to them, "Good morning, I am humbled and honored to be here with you today to commemorate a man whose courage and resolve helped change the course of history, but I ask you not to judge me by the color of my skin or the title that I hold, but as your sister in Christ, who loves each and every one of you."

The atmosphere shifted, I felt genuine love and appreciation from the audience, and then I delivered the speech that I believe God had for me to give:

> "*Once to every man and nation comes the moment to decide in the strife of truth with falsehood for the good or evil side.*[1]

"Dr. Martin Luther King, Jr. was that man who, in his moment of decision, chose to stand for truth and the side of good. Over the last few weeks, I have spent some time re-listening to several of Dr. King's speeches. And, I am so moved by the man and servant-leader he was. He was a man with incredible passion, a heart for justice, and a strong commitment to nonviolence. But there has been another aspect of his life and legacy that has really convicted me.

"On April 3, 1968, one day before he was assassinated, Dr. King gave a speech in which he said, "Like anybody, I would like to live a long life. Longevity has its place. But I'm not concerned about that now. I just want to do God's will."

"This was his moment of decision, and I am so struck by the similarities to Someone Else who was willing to lay down His own desires, His own will, and ultimately His own life for the sake of other people, for the sake of being obedient to God.

"Martin Luther King Jr. modeled his Savior and Lord Jesus Christ by abandoning his own well-being, his own safety, and his own will. He chose to bear the cross of injustice, persecution, and suffering.

In honor of fifty years of Dr. King's legacy, I am challenging myself and our country today with these questions. What are you willing to lay down your life for? What are we willing to lay down our lives for? Are we willing to be that one to persevere and struggle on behalf of the greater good? Do we value the will of God and the well-being of our brothers and sisters all of whom have been made in the image of God and have come from one tribe and one loving Father, above our own will?

"In that final speech, Dr. King said he was not afraid because he had been to the mountaintop and seen the Promised Land. Now he is in the real Promised Land with his Savior Jesus Christ. While we have made great strides, we still have miles to go to the promised land of racial justice. To quote Dr. King, "Justice is love correcting that which revolts against love."

This is where I pivoted and changed my ending. The Holy Spirit prompted me to say this:

"What I am about to say is not in my speech, but I feel led to share a personal, private moment I had this week. In my quiet time, I was reading Dr. King's 'Letter from a Birmingham Jail,' and when I read where he had to explain to his six-year-old daughter why she couldn't go to the public amusement park because it was closed to colored children, I just cried my eyes out that anyone from my race would ever treat someone of another race this way. I am so sorry. I am sorry, and I want you to know from the bottom of my heart how sorry I am, and I love each and every one of you."

To my surprise, I received a standing ovation from the majority of the crowd. Given how hostile the environment had felt at the beginning of my speech, I wasn't even expecting anyone to clap. So, God is the One who really deserved that standing ovation because His heart truly came into mine for the people who were there and had experienced such pain because of the color of their skin.

At the end of the service, I had so many African Americans come up to me, thank me, and hug me. Even as I was walking back to my car, people on the street who had watched it on television asked me if I was the woman who had given the speech. It was a very emotional day. One I will never forget. It showed me the power of admitting injustice, the power of acknowledging the wounds of racism, and the power of love to break down walls. People really are willing to look for the best in others.

One person can make a difference, just like Dr. Martin Luther King, Jr. His decision to stand up for righteousness and truth changed the course of history. We now have that same choice. Will you join Alveda and me in being a bold voice of healing and unity to bridge the racial divide? I pray you will say "yes" and answer that call, and together we can build bridges and heal broken hearts.

Reflection: What would it look like for you to be bolder when it comes to standing up for injustice?

—PRAYER—

Dear Heavenly Father, thank You for the boldness of Dr. King and his righteous convictions. We pray that You would help us seek You to equip us with the resilience, courage, and love that You gave to Dr. King and so many who served alongside him in the fight for civil rights. We ask You to help us carry on his legacy of sacrifice. Help each of us put ourselves in one another's shoes and see from their perspective. Help us to listen and be willing to ask for forgiveness when needed. Give us humble hearts to love as You love, in Jesus's name, Amen.

Alveda Speaks

From Ginger's testimony above, we can see once again that love never fails. Ginger's position of repentance, forgiveness, and agape love speaks to God's pattern for racial healing and reconciliation. I must admit once again that this occasion was very difficult for me to sit through because of the barbs and political jabs. While I was not a featured speaker for the King Week church service that day in 2018, I was sitting on the front row among family members during the event. Tensions were high, to say the least.

Ginger was seated on the platform with a group of people who were primarily diametrically politically opposed to her worldview. Of course, there were others on the stage who shared her values. Dr. Ben Carson, for example, was a featured speaker. Interestingly enough, he also spoke of love and forgiveness, which won for him affirming 'amens' from the audience.

Looking back, I can see that the only message which is truly aligned with that of Uncle ML, as well as that of my father, my grandfather, grandmother, and indeed every member of our King Family Legacy is the message of agape love, which encompasses repentance, forgiveness, and God's love.

One common theme with the MLK religious services every year is that of unity among the nations. Regardless of skin hue, every nation and every tribe are always included. Even when I don't always agree with the manmade themes from year to year, I am always blessed by the performances of the youth and young people who contribute with dance, song, artistry, and theatrical contributions of every sort. It is heartwarming to see that their varying skin hues and ethnic costumes do not divide them. They get it; skin color does not designate our race as individuals. Our one blood does that.

Reflection: What color is love?

—PRAYER—

Dear Heavenly Father, in Jesus's name, please help us to look deeper, beyond our skin color to discover the truth about Your plan for racial reconciliation.

https://youtu.be/-kksykAiL24

LET FREEDOM RING

Chapter Eight

COLORBLIND? WHY NOT?

———————◆———————

He replied, 'Whether he is a sinner or not,
I don't know.
One thing I do know is
I was blind but now I see!

—John 9:25—

———————◆———————

"THAT OLD LAW ABOUT 'AN EYE FOR AN EYE'
LEAVES EVERYBODY BLIND.
THE TIME IS ALWAYS RIGHT
TO DO THE RIGHT THING."

—Dr. Martin Luther King Jr. —

Alveda Speaks

"Trump is a racist."

"Kanye is a coon."

"We need to be colorblind."

"The races need to unite."

Sound familiar?

Currently, racial tension among the human family is at fever pitch. Here at home in the United States of America, tempers are flaring and emotions are boiling over the skin-color war. Can we take a timeout, please?

Acts 17:26 clearly teaches us that we are of one blood, one human race. Yet, for thousands of years, skin color wars, religious disputes, and class and caste disputes have divided the human family. For the purpose of this chapter, let's address only the skin-color factor that breeds the lie of separate races and racism.

In the realm of sociology, colorblindness is a concept based upon ignoring or pretending not to see the color of a person's skin. Colorblindness is a premise describing a desired ideal of a society where racial classifications do not exist to limit a person's opportunities. In seeking such race-neutral policies, proponents seek to promote the goal of racial equality. This ideal was promulgated to Frederick Douglass in the nineteenth century, and to the supporters of the twentieth century civil rights movement as well as in international antiracist movements of the 1950s and 1960s.

The challenge to these efforts is that, while well-meaning, abolition-minded citizens were genuinely seeking to bring unity and equality to all people, there were those who were seeking to actively and aggressively continue the racial and social inequities that would provide superiority to various people groups; communities divided by skin color and other socioeconomic factors.

Sometimes good intentions pave the way to hell. While hiding behind the guise of "good intentions," people sometimes knowingly or unknowingly attempt to maintain a "status quo" of communities divided by skin color and other socioeconomic factors.

Ironically, this colorblind issue isn't just an American concern. The skin color debate isn't limited to just those who identified as "black" or "white." Red, yellow, and brown complexions are also engaged in spiritual and emotional conflicts over the misunderstanding about skin color. Oddly, the more we pretend not to see skin color, the larger the elephant in the room becomes.

While there isn't enough time to address this phenomenon in depth, you, dear reader, might want to take the time to discuss skin color dilemmas that manifest in many cultures. We discussed Queen Sophie from England in chapter two. Now, let's look to the far east. Search for "The Comfort Women," and "The Silk Road." You will discover that the skin color battle knows no bounds.

The goal of 1960s civil rights legislation in the United States was to replace racial discrimination with a race-neutral standard. Reverend Martin Luther King Jr.'s central hope was that people would someday be judged by "the content of their character" rather than "the color of their skin." This dream has never truly been realized because the skin color issues keep getting in the way.

Skin-color racism is at the heart of the sin of rebellion against the Word of God that we are one race/one blood. As we battle with the three-headed monster of racism, reproductive genocide, and sexual perversion, we can see that skin color racism is a factor in these factions. Think about it: if someone is not the same "race" as you, they don't matter as much to you. You may even secretly consider them less than you; so much so that you can excuse injustices based upon the perceived classification of humanity.

Friends, we are faced with a 3 headed
monster that resists the Word of the Lord –
"Be fruitful and multiply" (procreate)!

Racism: No mating with
"inferior" humans who are
not my "color".

RACISM

SEXUAL
PERVERSION

Homosexuality
Fornication
Adultery
Incest
Other Hidden Practices
Human Trafficking
Pornography

Reproductive
Genocide

Abortion
And
Unnatural Contraception:
No babies born.
Women maimed:
Babies slaughtered

INTERESTING DOT-CONNECTING FACTS THAT DEFEND THE POSITION OF NOT BEING COLORBLIND

- Remember, there is only one human race. As human beings, our "race" is defined by our red blood and not our skin color.

- We should be judged by the content of our character rather than our visual, easily discerned physical characteristics such as the color of our skin, which we can see with our natural eyes.

- Colorblind is a medical, soulish, or spiritual condition requiring healing. Jesus gives sight to the blind.

- There is no such thing as interracial marriage or biracial sexual connections between humans because we are one human race.

- Upon conception or fertilization, the baby created from the sexual union is a human being because the parents are human beings.

- In the United States, practices such as redlining, discriminatory lending practices, and color-selective benefits are all part of a form of generational racism that receives a blind eye. For example, Veterans Day celebrates the GI Bill legislation that helped millions of returning veterans go to college and buy homes in the great postwar suburban land rush. Unfortunately, America often turns a blind eye to the seamy side of this story, which is how a largely disproportionate number of African American veterans, because of their skin color, were intentionally denied many of the benefits of the GI Bill. Practices such as these laid the foundation for what is known as "white privilege" in America today, where blacks are still subjected to racist conditions in the justice, education, health, and economic systems.[1]

• The use of census data, social security numbers, and zip codes in a system (aka "white privilege" or "redlining") is still used today to selectively control predatory lending practices, with people being judged by the color of their skin rather than the contents of their bank accounts.[2]

• Colorblindness is a passive form of racism. If you can't see color, you can also ignore the racist effects that are often amplified by active racists. If we are ethnically colorblind, we need a spiritual magnifying glass.

• See skin color and embrace it as a beautiful gift from God. As human beings, we are all created in living color.

Reflection: Are there things about skin color I now need to see that were not clear before?

—PRAYER—

Dear Heavenly Father, please open my eyes that I may see Your plans for Your human creation. In Jesus's name, Amen.

Ginger Speaks

In light of discussing racism, the term colorblind initially sounds like a really good thing, and you might ask, "Why should I not be colorblind? Didn't Martin Luther King Jr. use the famous phrase that we should judge people on the content of their character rather than the color of their skin?"

There is a wonderful article in *Psychology Today* by Dr. Monnica T. Williams that so eloquently discusses this very issue.

"Let's break it down into simple terms: Color-Blind = 'People of color, we don't see you (at least not that bad "colored" part).' As a person of color, I like who I am, and I don't want any aspect of that to be seen or invisible. The need for colorblindness implies there is something shameful about the way God made me and the culture I was born into that we shouldn't talk about. Thus, colorblindness has helped make race into a taboo topic that polite people cannot openly discuss. And if you can't talk about it, you can't understand it, much less fix the racial problems that plague our society.[1]"

As a Caucasian, I readily admit that I have been colorblind in the past. To be blind means that you cannot see, and I want to be able to see. I *need* to be able to see and recognize that a person's race dramatically impacts their life experiences. For instance, I had a conversation with a friend recently about how many young African American children do not have the luxury of safely playing outside of their homes because of the crime in their neighborhoods. On the flip side, many Caucasian children grow up playing in their front yards and community parks without any fear of danger. In the South, African Americans are statistically more likely to live in poverty than Caucasians are, and generational racism has undoubtedly played a role in this. So, I want to be able to appreciate the beauty of different cultures but also see the painful effects of racial discrimination. Unless you and I are able to see people and their life experiences clearly, we cannot heal the great divide.

Though there have been generations of Americans that have engaged in slavery, segregation, and racism, we have the opportunity to be the generation that rejects all division amongst people groups and turns the tide. In Deuteronomy 5:10, God says He will show "love to a thousand generations of those who love Me and keep My commandments" (NIV). Did you get that? Our wonderful Father God says that He shows His love to a thousand generations of those who love Him and keep His commandments. Let's be the generation in America that passes on the gift of blessings to our future generations for at least a thousand years by the ways we love each other and our God!

It's important for us to ask the Holy Spirit to reveal all biases and judgments in our own hearts that we have towards people who look, act, and live differently than us. Unfortunately, prejudice has the ability to condition us to make broad assumptions about many things, especially different ethnic groups. In order to truly love each other, we must first confront our own biases and then seek to engage with people who come from other cultures to better understand people's stories. In order to truly love someone, you must know them. And in order to truly know them, you must be familiar with the unique burdens they bear and experiences they've lived. In order to be acquainted with these attributes, you have to acknowledge that color, socioeconomic status, gender, age, culture, etc., shape who people are and impact their identity.

None of us chooses the color of our skin, but it is God who gave us our skin color and determines our ethnicity. And none of us gets to choose the history of our ancestors, nor the family we are born into. Thus, while we can't undo the sins nor the suffering of our forefathers, we must acknowledge our history and be determined to pursue justice in our society for generations to come.

A turning point in my life has been acknowledging that race has undoubtedly impacted the daily realities of African Americans in our country. We cannot overlook the enduring pain of our brothers and sisters of color and say that we walk in the love of Christ. As we commit to racial reconciliation, the first thing we must do is open our eyes to see the living colors we were all created with and appreciate the beauty our Heavenly Father has displayed in each and every shade of His children.

If you have been guilty of being colorblind, I invite you to make this declaration and say this prayer with me now: "Father God, I recognize my shortcomings and blindness to my own sin and the tendency of my flesh to make judgments about people because of the color of their skin. I acknowledge the pain and the racial injustices that have existed in our country, and I pray for generational wounds to be healed in Jesus's Name. I take full responsibility for my own heart, and I pray You would use me to be a part of the solution to racism in our country. Open my eyes to see each person as You see them. I declare from this day forward I will strive to live in harmony and unity with all of the human race regardless of skin color. I will appreciate our differences and see others as You see them. In Jesus's Name, Amen."

Reflection: In what ways have you been colorblind? Now that you see clearly, what step will you take to bridge the gap between the races?

—PRAYER—

Dear Heavenly Father, thank You that You created all of us in Your image. You created us to be different in color, language, and culture. But You want us to appreciate the unique differences in one another and see what is so special about each and every human being. Forgive us for being colorblind. Open our eyes so that we may glorify You by seeing in living color, appreciating the beauty and life in those around us. In Jesus's name, Amen.

Chapter Nine

LIVING TOGETHER AS BROTHERS AND SISTERS

"WE MUST LEARN TO LIVE TOGETHER AS BROTHERS OR PERISH TOGETHER AS FOOLS."[1]

—Dr. Martin Luther King Jr.—

The King will reply, 'Truly I tell you, whatever you did for one of the least of these brothers and sisters of mine, you did for Me.'

—Matthew 25:40 (NIV—

How pleasant it is when brothers live together in unity.

—Psalm 133:1 (NIV—

Ginger Speaks

Since Alveda and I are sisters in Christ writing this book together, I am going to add to Dr. King's quote and say, "We must learn to live together as brothers *and sisters*, or perish together as fools."[1]

If we are going to learn to live together, we have to start treating each other as family. As the saying goes, people don't care how much you know until they know how much you care. We need to begin building relationships, not pitting one group against the other. That may sound very lofty, but how do we practically build relationships and start living together as brothers and sisters?

The above Scripture from Matthew 25 is a good starting point. Jesus is talking about the End Times when He will come back in all His glory and judge the nations. In Matthew 25:34–40, He says,

Then the King will say to those on his right, 'Come, you who are blessed by my Father; take your inheritance, the kingdom prepared for you since the creation of the world. For I was hungry and you gave me something to eat, I was thirsty and you gave me something to drink, I was a stranger and you invited me in, I needed clothes and you clothed me, I was sick and you looked after me, I was in prison and you came to visit me.'

'Then the righteous will answer him, "Lord, when did we see you hungry and feed you, or thirsty and give you something to drink? When did we see you a stranger and invite you in, or needing clothes and clothe you? When did we see you sick or in prison and go to visit you?" The King will reply, 'Truly I tell you, whatever you did for one of the least of these brothers and sisters of mine, you did for me.'

(NIV)

It is important how we treat others because how we treat others is actually how we treat Jesus. Wow! Let that sink in for a moment. These aren't my words; they're His. What if every day we purposed in our hearts to treat each person we come in contact with as if he or she were the Lord Himself? What would our homes, businesses, churches, cities, nations, and world look like?

Jesus was and is the ultimate servant-leader. He led by serving, so we should emulate Him and treat everyone as our brothers and sisters in love.

Now, I am the oldest of two brothers, and I can tell you that growing up, we had our share of sibling squabbles. What family doesn't have those? But at the end of the day, we resolved our conflicts and grew to love and appreciate each other even more. We may not always agree, and many times we may agree to disagree, but we love each other. We will always have differences between us. But if we show each other genuine respect, then we can live together in harmony as brothers and sisters.

In reflecting upon the issue of racism in our nation, I was reminded of the Bible story of David triumphing over the giant Goliath. I believe racism is a giant in our country, and we need to slay it! At one Republican National Committee meeting, I gave a talk on slaying giants in our lives, and I believe it is applicable for how we can conquer prejudice in our hearts. My three points were that we are called, we are equipped, and we are surrendered. We are called by God; therefore, He equips us with the tools we need. Then, we must surrender to Him to work through us. Since God has called us to the ministry of reconciliation, including racial reconciliation, He will equip us with what we need to accomplish this great task. When we surrender to His Holy Spirit, He will lead us into unity.

Alveda and I are sisters in Christ, and we want to come alongside our brothers and sisters of all ethnicities to defeat the giant of racism. David had five smooth stones when he killed Goliath in the Old Testament. Let's ask God to give us the stones we need to knock down the giant of racism and cut off its ugly head!

Reflection: Giants inherently are intimidating. What about the giant of racism is most intimidating or challenging in your mind, and why?

—PRAYER—

Dear Heavenly Father, You made us all to live together as brothers and sisters, not to perish together as fools. Help us learn to see each other through the eyes of compassion, kindness, mercy, and grace. Give us hearts to share one another's burdens and trials. Help us to rejoice with others' happiness and grieve with them in their sorrows. Give us the boldness to slay the giant of racism and be united as one loving family made up of all cultures and creeds. Help us to learn from Jesus who truly showed us how to love. In Jesus's name, Amen.

Alveda Speaks

But He said to them in reply, 'Who are my mother and my brothers?' And looking around at those seated in the circle He said, 'Here are my mother and my brothers. For whoever does the will of God is my brother and sister and mother.' — Mark 3:31-35

Obviously, in Mark 3:31–35, Jesus is not speaking of post-Adamic natural and biological siblings; in other words, brothers and sisters born of mutual parents, or sharing the same mother and/or father. So, when we speak of acknowledging that we are all related as human beings and living together as brothers and sisters, we are not just speaking esoterically. Actually, if we were to go back to the Garden of Eden, we could find scientific evidence that supports the one-blood theory of Acts 17:26. We actually are all related, of one blood, and sharing the same DNA profiles from the beginning. However, in Mark 3:31–35, Jesus was speaking of spiritual relations.

We recently moved into a blended community where people of all ages, sizes, shapes, and skin colors reside. For most of my life, I've lived in neighborhoods that were predominantly comprised of African American families, so this has been a new and very rewarding experience for me. On both sides of our house, the homes of our neighbors juxtapose with ours. We talk over the fence like they used to do in the 1980s television shows. Neighbors actually show up at the door with cupcakes and baskets of fruit. My grandchildren make artsy-crafty gifts for the neighbors. They all frolic together in the community pool. Red and yellow, black and white—all are precious in God's sight. And, it's all right here in our neighborhood.

Before I left "the other side of town" and as I was sharing that I was "moving north," people reacted in many different ways: "They might be racist up there," or "Are you getting uppity, too good for our kind?" Wow! Really? In today's world?

As the days, hours, and minutes ticked by and the boxes were being packed and set by the door, I remember remarking to my family how more and more people of every ethnic blend were shopping at "our stores." The ethnicities of the moviegoers and staff at the local movie theater were becoming more blended. So, God was preparing me for my new home; and, not just the one here on Earth, but also the eternal one in heaven.

Once, not so very long ago, it became popular to be able to say things like, "I have a white friend. I have a black friend, or Asian friend, or Latino friend," and on and on and on. Finally, the question arose, and is still being asked, "Is there only one?" Why must we divide our communities by color, socioeconomic, or even religious distinctions?

For followers of Christ, our greatest strength is in our love for God and for each other. This love, when genuine, flows across every barrier, melting even the hardest of hearts. Ginger and I have resolved to put aside skin color differences and celebrate our God-given designs in harmony. We are not colorblind; we are sisters in Christ!

My friendship with Ginger is evidence that it is possible to have a strong and genuine relationship with a person of another race that is not defined by skin color. While I do see her skin color, I also see her as a friend and a sister in Christ. As Ginger explained, the inspiration for this book was her prophetic dream about us writing together. Over the months that we have labored together with this project, our friendship has grown stronger. As you read this, I challenge you to see every person beyond their race, and as a human being. How hard can that be?

Reflection: What color is love? This question may seem redundant, but how has your perspective changed since you began reading this book? Are you ready to lay aside skin color barriers and see people through new eyes?

—PRAYER—

Dear Heavenly Father, thank You for bringing the points in this book to our attention so that we can share and share alike the truth that we are designed to be Your children. In Jesus's name, Amen.

*We can explore all of the scientific evidence;
we can read all of the writings of the great
philosophers. Yet, at the end of the day, we
come back to the point of agape love. We are
human beings, created in the image of God,
regardless of skin color. We are one human
race, created by a loving God.*

—Dr. Alveda King—

Chapter Ten

ONE BLOOD,
ONE HUMAN RACE

———◉———

*From one blood God made all people, [so] that they should
inhabit the whole earth; and God marked out their appointed
times in history and the boundaries of their lands. God did this
so that they would seek God and perhaps reach out for God and
find God, though God is not far from any one of us. 'For in God
we live and move and have our being.' As some of your own
poets have said, 'We are God's offspring.'*

—Acts 17:26-28 (NIV)—

———◉———

Ginger Speaks

This Scripture speaks volumes, and it is one I hear my sweet
sister, Alveda, quote often when discussing racism. It is Truth,
but how do we practically live this out? All people that have been

born on this earth, tracing all the way back to our first parents in the Garden of Eden, Adam and Eve, came from one blood. God made all of us in His image to be His image bearers and to dwell together in unity. But even our first family didn't get it right, and it's been downhill ever since Eve believed the serpent's lie and ate the forbidden fruit.

After sin entered the world, we all have been alienated from God and at war with each other. Division has plagued the human race from the beginning, even with Adam and Eve's son, Cain, who became so jealous of his brother, Abel, that he murdered him.

Knowing that humanity would need a Savior to bridge the gap between God and His people, He made a plan that would be fulfilled thousands of years later by having His one and only Son leave the glories of heaven and come to the earth. Jesus was conceived miraculously by the Holy Spirit in a teenaged girl who was engaged to be married. Thankfully, her fiancé, Joseph, didn't have her stoned nor call off the engagement because an angel of God appeared to him in a dream and told him that she really was carrying the Messiah conceived by the Holy Spirit. Jesus was born with one mission and purpose: to grow up to die for the sins of the whole human race.

It still boggles my mind that Jesus would love me so much that He would take my place and take all my sin upon Himself so that I might be made righteous in the eyes of God. Since Jesus bore the consequences of my sin *and* my family iniquities, I no longer have to live under condemnation. Instead, I live under the freedom of knowing I am truly forgiven and have been made clean through His death on the cross. Jesus died for everyone: slave traders, prostitutes, tax collectors, Pharisees, murderers, liars, drunkards, child molesters, and every sinner ever born and to be born. He died for you, and He died for me.

Contrary to popular belief, we cannot earn our way to heaven. Christianity is not a religion; it is a relationship. Every other religion tries to work its way up to God, but Christianity is the opposite because Christ came down to us. He bridged the great divide. He bore our shame so that we don't have to. In Jesus' death on the cross, He forgave our sins so that we have the opportunity to be at peace with God through Him. The gospel means "good news." And it is good news that once we get our relationship right with God, we are then empowered to have healthy relationships with others.

If Jesus, who is perfect in every way, can show forgiveness to us when we are so undeserving of it, how can we not extend the same forgiveness to others? We ask Jesus to forgive us of all our sins to have a relationship with Him, and we then learn how to love and forgive others because of what He demonstrated for us. How can we say we are Christians and love the Lord who we can't see, and at the same time not love our brothers and sisters who we can see? (1 John 4:20). This doesn't make sense, and it grieves the Lord. He wants us to show the world our love for Him by showing one another His love for us. And in order to do this, we have to learn to ask for forgiveness and to forgive.

Through Christ's example, we have seen that true love involves unmerited forgiveness and grace, and we can now emulate Jesus in how we treat *all* of our brothers and sisters. There needs to be more love, real love, God's love; true sacrificial love. In order to have real healing amongst people of different races, we are going to have to make sacrifices for each other. When people feel loved and valued, they can let their defenses down, open up, and listen to someone else who may differ from them. I love our country, and it grieves me deeply to see such division along ethnic and political lines. As a country, we are either going to grow together or grow apart, and it is my heartfelt prayer, as it is Alveda's, that we begin to grow together and truly be one nation under God.

Reflection: In this chapter, I have explained what it takes to have a relationship with God. And I realize that not everyone has made this decision. If you feel the Holy Spirit has stirred your heart, then I am writing out a simple prayer for you to ask Jesus to forgive you of your sins so that you, too, can be reconciled to God. Below is a prayer of salvation.

—PRAYER—

Dear Lord Jesus, I realize that my sins have separated me from You. I am truly sorry for my sins, and I ask You to forgive me now of all of my family sins and iniquities and all the ways that I have personally sinned against You. I am sorry for the things I have done wrong in my life. Thank You for dying on the cross for me so that I could be forgiven and restored to You. I receive Your forgiveness and ask You to come into my heart and be Lord over all of my life. Thank You, Lord Jesus. Amen.

Alveda Speaks

Throughout the book I have written about the science of the one blood commonality among humans—how we are all really one race and one blood. Following Ginger's lead now, I speak of the spiritual reality of the one human blood that unites us here on Earth, and then the supernatural blood of Jesus that connects us to God as our Father throughout eternity.

If we will relax from our dependence on traditions of man and allow our hearts and mind to understand some of the mysteries of God, then we might be able to agree that we are one blood, one human race. If we can arrive at this understanding, then we may be ready and able to understand the even stronger kinship available to us through the blood of Jesus.

Consider this. We sing a song with these familiar lyrics, "The blood that Jesus shed for me... It will never lose its power."[1] Do we really know what we are singing?

According to the Bible, a child is the seed of its father, not the mother. Still, the child gains part of the mother's looks and maternal DNA because she provides the egg, which contains her DNA. So, the child is the product of both parents. However, the seed comes from the father; the child is considered whatever the father is. If we can accept and believe by faith that, because Jesus had no blood from a human father or mother, he was born sinless; that is, without generational sin or disease.

The extensive research of Martin R. DeHaan, MD explains how "He who knew no sin [Jesus]" was able to deliver us from our sins:

"The Bible teaches in addition that Jesus was a sinless man. While all men [people] from Adam to this day are born [of one blood – Acts 17:26] with Adam's sinful nature, and, therefore, are subject to the curse and eternal death, the Man Jesus was without sin and, therefore, deathless until He took the sin of others upon Himself and died their death. Now while Jesus was of Adam's [one blood] race according to the flesh, yet He did not inherit Adam's nature. This alone will prove that sin is not transmitted through the flesh. It is transmitted through the blood and not the flesh, and even though Jesus was of the "Seed of David according to the flesh" this could not make him a sinner...

It is now definitely known that the blood which flows in an unborn babies' arteries and veins is not derived from the mother but is produced within the body of the fetus itself only after the introduction of the male sperm. An unfertilized ovum can never develop blood since the female egg does not by itself contain the elements essential for the production of this blood. It is only after the male element has entered the ovum that blood can develop... From the time of conception to the time of birth of the infant not *one single drop of blood* ever passes from mother to child..."[2]

This phenomenon does not negate the role of the mother in the formation of the unique birth of every human being. There are significant and lasting links to mothers and their children that are evident in every birth and, indeed, in every life in the womb of its mother. Even abortion and miscarriages do not sever these bonds. Children remain linked to their mothers through "ghost cells," which can lend uncanny connections between mothers and their children.[3] Certain trauma such as abortion, miscarriage, and abuse is suspected to cause lasting impacts in mothers who can suffer cases of fibromyalgia and other conditions that are difficult to diagnose.[4]

The link between a mother and child is profound, and new research suggests a physical connection even deeper than anyone thought. The profound psychological and physical bonds shared by the mother and her child begin during gestation when the mother is everything for the developing fetus, supplying warmth and sustenance, while her heartbeat provides a soothing constant rhythm.

The physical connection between mother and fetus is provided by the placenta, an organ, built of cells from both the mother and fetus, which serves as a conduit for the exchange of nutrients, gasses, and wastes. Cells may migrate through the placenta between the mother and the fetus, taking up residence in many organs of the body including the lung, thyroid, muscle, liver, heart, kidney and skin. These may have a broad range

161

of impacts, from tissue repair and cancer prevention to sparking immune disorders.

It is remarkable that it is so common for cells from one individual to integrate into the tissues of another distinct person.[5]

Understanding these mysteries that are being revealed to us at this time in history, it becomes increasingly important for us to learn to come together as the one blood human race so that we can be blessed by the transformational blood of Jesus.

In Psalm 8:4, the question is asked: "What is mankind that you are mindful of them, human beings that you care for them?" As we follow that line of reasoning, we can ask: Is humanity defined by blood type, by skin color, or by DNA? Or is there more to what we are? We can explore all of the scientific evidence; we can read all of the writings of the great philosophers. Yet, at the end of the day, we come back to the point of agape love. We are human beings, created in the image of God, regardless of skin color. We are one human race, created by a loving God.

Reflection: How can we prepare our hearts and minds to receive more truth?

Please pray the following prayer with us. Rededicate your life to Christ if you have already prayed and received God's grace.

—Prayer—

Dear Lord Jesus, I realize that my sins have separated me from You. I am truly sorry for my sins and I ask You to forgive me now of all of my family sins and iniquities and all the ways that I have personally sinned against God. I am sorry for the things I have done wrong in my life. Thank You for dying on the cross for me that I could be forgiven and restored to You. I receive Your forgiveness and ask You to come into my heart and be Lord over all of my life. Thank You, Lord Jesus. Amen.

(As you might notice, Ginger and I used the same prayer in this chapter, even though we didn't consult each other about it. There must be a divine reason we both felt compelled to include this particular "sinner's prayer," so we intentionally decided to keep it in the book twice.)

We can come together to end the dark sins of racism
and prejudice, and we can heal the divide that
many of us have not wanted to confront.
In fighting the darkness with His light,
we become Jesus's ambassadors.

—Ginger Howard—

Chapter Eleven

LET THE LIGHT SHINE

"Darkness cannot drive out darkness;
only light can do that.
Hate cannot drive out hate;
only love can do that."

—Dr. Martin Luther King Jr.—

Arise, shine; For your light has come!
And the glory of the Lord is risen upon you.

—Isaiah 60:1 (NIV)—

But if we walk in the light,
as He is in the light,
we have fellowship with one another…

—1 John 1:7a (NIV)—

Ginger Speaks

LIGHT ALWAYS OVERCOMES DARKNESS

Jesus is the light of the world. When we follow Him, we have His light because He lives in us. In John 8:12, He explains this by saying, "I am the light of the world. Whoever follows me will never walk in darkness, but will have the light of life" (NIV). Jesus also tells us in Matthew 5:14, "*You* are the light of the world. A town built on a hill that cannot be hidden" (NIV, emphasis added). Light always overcomes darkness.

We are to carry the light of Jesus out into a dark and dreary world, and when we do, the light overtakes the darkness. We can come together to end the dark sins of racism and prejudice, and we can heal the divide that many of us have not wanted to confront. In fighting the darkness with His light, we become Jesus's ambassadors.

To be perfectly honest, in my naiveté, I didn't realize what a divide there was until I went to the Beloved Community Talks and the Martin Luther King Jr. Day Commemoration Service in 2018. I recognized the division, and I was convicted by the racism that still exists in our country and wanted to be a part of shedding light on this reality. I want people to know that I truly care, and I want a solution for this. I don't think one book will change everything, but it will continue a conversation, and we have to talk more.

We also need to learn how to hear one another! There's a difference between listening and hearing. You can listen all day long, but unless you HEAR what someone else is saying, nothing is going to improve.

The Lord is the only One who brings reconciliation. We have to line all of this up with God. He shows us the way. In fact, John 14:6 says this, "Jesus answered, 'I am the way and the truth and the life. No one comes to the Father except through Me'" (NIV).

With Him as our guide, we can start conversations and continue the process of healing. I say *continue* because we have made great strides, thanks to the sacrifices of Dr. Martin Luther King Jr. and Alveda's father, the Reverend A. D. King, and many others who have gone before us and paved the way. They let their light shine in the darkest of nights, yet their earthly light was snuffed out too early because of the cause they believed in and ultimately died for. I am looking forward to meeting them in heaven and thanking them for the sacrifices they made so that our country could be a better place.

I am grateful for my precious friend and sister in Christ, Alveda, who has co-labored with me in this endeavor of letting light shine on the darkness of racism. Her light shines brightly every day. She is constantly showing God's love to all who hear her whether on FOX News or in her work advocating for the lives of the unborn. Her uncle and her father would be so proud of her for standing up for the civil rights of those who cannot speak for themselves.

In writing this book, our hope has been to shed light on some of the darkness in our country that historically has not been confronted with the appropriate conviction and attention. Racism still is a dark stain on the fabric of this great nation. Although slavery has ended and Jim Crow laws have been abolished, true reconciliation has not been achieved. Our prayer is that these pages stir healing and reconciliation in the hearts of all who read them, bringing light that reveals truth and leads to societal transformation. Our desire is that this book would be one positive step toward truly living together as brothers and sisters, recognizing the beauty in our different ethnicities and cultures. We are not colorblind, and we hope that by now, you're not either!

Reflection: What are some practical ways you can be a light for social justice and racial reconciliation in your community?

—PRAYER—

Dear Heavenly Father, thank You that You are the Light of the world. And when You live in us and allow Yourself to shine Your light through us, darkness cannot abide. Lord, I pray that Your light would shine so brightly in and through us that we would truly see the beauty of each person made in the image of God, love them with an unconditional love, and celebrate who You created them to be. In Jesus's name, Amen.

Alveda Speaks

At their best, the generosity and kindness of the human spirit are exceeded only by the complete sovereign love of God. Before the transformation of the human spirit by the entering in of the Holy Spirit, it is only the inherent nature of the person that drives the deeds and actions. Nature and nurture play a part in this process. However, when the light of God shines into our hearts, day breaks and we begin to shine.

Have you ever heard a person say, or maybe even you have said yourself, "I like the way I am. I don't want to change?" Well, my pastor, Theo Allen McNair Jr., often says, "Am can change."

Perhaps you have been seeing and defining yourself as a member of a specific race rather than being part of an ethnic nation or tribe. You may have convinced yourself, or at least been taught, that you are part of a specific race of humans. However, the Word of God says that you are created of one blood. If you believe God's Word, then you can change your mindset to the position of being a member of the one-blood human race.

Once unity comes, we will be able to conquer anything as long as we continue together in faith, hope, and love. Here are some notes from my personal approach to living at peace with God and the world:

1. Do not get out of bed without your spiritual armor of God! Stay in the Spirit, and be guided by the Word of God. Satan has no place in the Spirit. His battleground is the flesh and the soul.

2. Start each day with prayer and Bible reading. Chapters from Psalms and the New Testament are a must. Also, daily reading is a stabilizing factor. Chapters from the Old Testament are also inspiring, insightful, and uplifting.

3. Resist the devil at all costs and refuse to enter into rebellion, unforgiveness, bitterness, and strife. Remember, "Love covers a multitude of sins."

4. Go to church. If you are not a member of a body where strong Bible teaching is going on, then find one. You must have spiritual food and fellowship.

5. Do not neglect your tithes and offerings. God will take care of your needs if you are obedient and give Him His due.

6. Be faithful in meeting your obligations at home, in your community, and at work. Pray without ceasing, work hard, and have fun. Your Christian light and example will win others to Christ. Give special attention to your roles as a spouse, parent, and sibling, and honor your parents!

7. Love and forgive your enemies so that our heavenly Father can forgive you. To walk in unforgiveness is a deadly hindrance to the light of God.

Reflection: The Lord will give you proper direction in prayer, and through your pastor and church leaders, as you continue in the battle. Remember, the battle is not ours but the Lord's, and through Him, we are more than conquerors! Are you ready to move ahead? God bless you.

—PRAYER—

The Lord Jesus prayed this prayer to His Father on our behalf:

"That they will all be one, just as you and I are one—as you are in me, Father, and I am in you. And may they be in us so that the world will believe you sent me" (John 17:21). Let us too pray for unity in the Lord. Amen.

From one man he made all the nations, that they should inhabit the whole earth; and he marked out their appointed times in history and the boundaries of their lands. God did this so that they would seek him and perhaps reach out for him and find him, though he is not far from any one of us. 'For in him we live and move and have our being. As some of your own poets have said, 'We are his offspring.'
—Acts 17:26-28—

Chapter Twelve

NEXT STEPS

Alveda Speaks

In 1967, Uncle ML wrote a book: WHERE DO WE GO FROM HERE: CHAOS OR COMMUNITY? There are no coincidences in the Kingdom of God. Everything is by His divine plan and will. Yet, it is simply fascinating to me that over five decades later, here I am, asking the same question. Where do we go from here, my friends? What are our next steps?

For starters, Ginger and I invite you to not only read our book, say our prayers with us, and reflect on the points we have shared, but we ask that you use this book as a starting point for many prayers and discussions of your own. Share your thoughts on social media. Overcome evil with good, with truth, and with light. Let the life of Jesus Christ burn bright in your circles; through you.

This book was birthed as a result of Ginger's dream which has been discussed earlier in previous sections. There was a two-year pause in our writing between the time of Ginger's dream and our initial submission to an agent to seek a publisher. During that time, much has happened. I'm amazed that God was not finished with us two years ago. Only God knew that there would be more to say before Dr. Clarice Fluitt would take us under her ministry wings and help us cross the finish line, publishing the book in 2020 just before the elections in the fall.

In July of 2020, civil rights leaders John Lewis and C. T. Vivian passed away on the same day, leaving a void in the atmosphere. I'm intentionally not discussing the political season here in this chapter. We put politics aside earlier in the book. I would like to mention, though, that there are new faces in the 2020 elections. I'll mention one 2020 candidate in particular who is very close to me; my goddaughter, Angela Stanton King. Ginger and I have had quite a ride in the 2020 political season. We have, maybe, never prayed harder.

As one who has been thrust into the forefront of the prayer campaigns of America from 2016-2020, I have been astounded by the increasing cries of the Christian community calling for America to return to God.

In the most recent days before the release of this book, here in 2020, we have experienced COVID-19, race wars, economic upheaval, and so much more trauma. Remarkably, while these occurrences have caused fear and panic among the people, there has been a responding surge of faith, hope, and love.

During the last few months, with the onset of COVID-19 and the 2020 race wars in America, the Acts 17:26-28 passage has literally jumped off the pages of the Bible and come to life all around us. When we started writing the book, it was as if we were pulling teeth; the breaking of fallow ground in a dry and barren land. Today, "one blood, one race" is on the lips of people far and wide. We are amazed and very grateful.

We can now see that from the beginning of our journey, God was and still is using the testimonies of Ginger and myself to unearth deeper truths, and to help to bring down that ancient demon of racism.

This last chapter is intentionally short. After all, we didn't even mean to publish more than ten chapters. Yet, God was not done with us. Neither is it over. Ginger and I will continue our journey together in the love of Christ. We hope to meet many of you along the way. God bless each and every one of you, as hearts and minds are changed, to embrace the love of God as one blood, one human race.

Reflection: One of my grandfather's favorite Scriptures is a key to your next steps:

> "Then the LORD answered me and said: "Write the vision and make it plain on tablets, that he may run who reads it" (Habakkuk 2:2).

Are you ready to start, or even finish a chapter in your own journal? If we were to consider that the Book of Acts in the Bible is a journal of sorts, would it be okay to suggest that each of us has a type of Book of our own Acts?

—PRAYER—

Dear Lord, thank You for the privilege of being used by You to write this book and to encourage and be encouraged along life's journeys. Thank You for my Christian Sister, Ginger Howard, and her companionship as a co-writer of this book. Please use the fruits of our labors for Your glory, as we learn to live together as brothers and sisters, loving each other Your way; never perishing as fools. In Jesus's Name, by the power of Your Holy Spirit. Amen.

Ginger Speaks

Tears are streaming down my face as I reflect on the end of this two-year endeavor and consider the blessing of Alveda's friendship. As we have journeyed together in writing this book, our love for each other has been cemented and strengthened, and I cherish the gift of our sisterhood now more than ever before. Reading Alveda's portion of the next steps, I really feel like there are no more words for me to add, but my sweet sister insisted that I give a final charge to you.

I am still in awe of God's timing. Although this book was supposed to be published and released two years ago, God kept allowing doors to shut in our faces. But now, in the midst of a national crisis where people are taking to the streets to have their voices heard, I can see the wisdom in God's perfect timing. I am so grieved by the pain and the deep racial wounds that have been exposed, and it is my prayer for this book to offer some hope and healing for our country in this season.

One of my favorite Scriptures is Romans 8:28, "And we know that in all things, God works for the good of those who love Him, who have been called according to His purpose." (NIV) And, after this long wait, I now know that God was waiting until this opportune time to release this book and start a conversation that might bring healing to our land. As I have said before in a previous chapter, I am not naive enough to believe that one book can be the solution for healing the racial divide, but I do believe it can be a useful tool to start the much needed conversation. Now more than ever, we need to lower our defenses, come together, and talk about ways to love our neighbor with racial reconciliation in mind.

So, my charge to you is to share this book with someone else, even just one other person, your family, your Bible study, or your colleagues at work, and to challenge yourself to consider how you may bridge the racial divide. Consider how you may put yourself in the shoes of someone who is totally different from you, and pursue friendships across ethnic lines to expand your perspective on how race has impacted your brothers and sisters. Ask yourself what the Lord would have you do to help bring healing to your office, your school, your city, and our country. There is so much that needs to be done, but I do believe that, as evidenced by Alveda's uncle, Dr. Martin Luther King Jr., one person can make a huge difference. My challenge to you is to be the one person who starts a healing conversation, cultivating empathy and fostering unity amongst all people.

Reflection: Spend some time meditating on this verse:

"Therefore if you have any encouragement from being united with Christ, if any comfort from his love, if any common sharing in the Spirit, if any tenderness and compassion, then make my joy complete by being like-minded, having the same love, being one in spirit and of one mind. Do nothing out of selfish ambition or vain conceit. Rather, in humility value others above yourselves, not looking to your own interests but each of you to the interests of the others" (Philippians 2:1-4 (NIV).

How might you apply this verse in your own season of life?

—PRAYER—

Dear Heavenly Father, thank You for this timely opportunity to shoulder this burden for our nation with my sweet sister Alveda. Lord, we ask You to use this book in the hands of each reader who picks it up. Please bless each person who reads these pages, and open their eyes to see and appreciate the colors displayed in every human being because You are the God of Creation, and You delight in every child You've made. Help all of us to realize that we can be the one voice that speaks life, healing, and unity. We ask all these things in the matchless name of Jesus Christ, Amen.

Jesus Christ calls us to a single identity as one body in one Lord, one faith, and one baptism. The stakes are high because without a common identity, true unity is not possible. Without true unity, love fails. Without love, it is impossible to keep the new commandment that Christ has given to all believers (John 12:34).

LAST WORD

Jarrett Ellis, Esq.

"Monkeys are superior to men in this: when a monkey looks into a mirror, he sees a monkey."

—Malcolm de Chazal—

———————◉———————

"Above all else, guard your heart, for everything you do flows from it."
—Proverbs 4:23—

———————◉———————

It is a tragic feature of human nature that all people, for all time, have in various ways struggled to truly understand what it means to be human. As Malcolm de Chazal mused, we too often see something less than human in others and more than human in ourselves, leading to distortions in the way that we think and behave. Sadly, the Church, and those who attempt to adhere to her teachings, are not immune. It is our hope that this volume may be useful toward the project of unraveling the confusion, and in so doing assist the Church in assuming a leadership role in influencing our culture on the important social issue of race relations rather than capitulating to prevailing norms.

We suggest that in order to effect change in our concepts and conversations concerning race, it is important to examine the history of the development of the idea of race within the Church until the present moment and how it does, or does not, align with Biblical precepts.

We begin by identifying the Bible's central descriptions of the nature of human beings. We first notice that human beings have a universal physical nature, marked by their ability to reproduce with one another (Genesis 1:28), resulting in an unbroken line of descent from our first parents, Adam and Eve (Acts 17:26) until the present day. Science has resoundingly confirmed the global relatedness of all people as reflected in the human genome and as visible in certain remarkable unique features and abilities, e.g., enlarged cerebral cortex and cerebellum, universal speech, upright posture, and hands with fully articulating digits, just to name a few. Indeed, no other species exhibits such biological and physiological unity across the planet as do humans, rendering the variations that we recognize within our species, like hair texture and eye color, unremarkable.

Far more important than the unique physicality of human beings are our unique mental and spiritual attributes. The Bible teaches us that God made humankind, male and female, in God's own image and likeness (Genesis 1:24). Because God is a spirit, this image and likeness, or the imago Dei, must refer to non-physical properties that are directly instilled by God into each human being at its creation. We understand that (i) God is love (1 John 4:16), and is therefore relational (Romans 1:21; Matthew 5:45; Colossians 1:15-20); (ii) God is moral and just (Psalm 97:2); (iii) God is the fount of all knowledge (Proverbs 2:6); (iv) and God is creative (Genesis 1). To be made in God's image and likeness therefore means that human beings are defined mentally and spiritually by (i) the ability to love and relate to God and His creation, (ii) the ability to recognize and honor universal morality and justice according to God's love, (iii) the ability to comprehend, in meaningful measure, the wisdom of God and receive the knowledge of God, and the (iv) the ability and responsibility to reflect and creatively express God's love, ethics, and wisdom, each according to his or her own unique formation by the hand of God. The combination of the physical kinship of humanity and shared mental/spiritual dimensions emanating directly from God distinguish humankind, globally, as a special creation, each equally precious in His sight (1 Corinthians 12:13).

The Church maintained the foregoing formulation for much of its history. Beginning with the earliest scholars from Irenaeus through Thomas Aquinas, Church doctrine maintained the solidarity of human identity imposed by our common origin in Adam and Eve, the equality of the spiritual nature in all people, to whatever ethnicity they belong, and by the redeeming sacrifice offered by Jesus Christ on behalf of all people to become the children of God.

Sadly, the long-held belief in the solidarity of human identity was substantially undermined in the 15th Century in the wake of social and political conflict originating in Europe and spreading to the New World. A watershed moment occurred on June 5, 1449, with the passage of the Sentencia-Estatuto, the first set of racial exclusion laws in modern history, in Toledo Spain. In the decades leading up to the Sentencia, Christians in Spain without direct Jewish, Muslim, or pagan ancestry (self-described as the "Old Christians") became increasingly distrustful of and hostile toward Christians who had converted from these heretical traditions (labeled the "New Christians"). Old Christians began accusing New Christians, particularly Jews, of secretly practicing Judaism and working against the Church according to the "perverse line of the Jews." In the wake of these hostilities arose the concept of the limpieza de sangre or "purity of blood," upon which the modern idea of race was founded. The phrase was understood literally, not figuratively, based on the medieval belief that blood played an essential role in establishing a person's character. The most sinister idea that resulted was the notion that although all human beings descended from Adam and Eve, certain character traits, abilities, tendencies, patterns of sin and righteousness, etc. were fixed in bloodlines that created a sort of unalterable hierarchy within Christendom. Pride in one's human bloodlines arose as a parallel theme with the redeeming blood of Christ.

The Bible clearly identifies the limpieza de sangre as unmitigated heresy, "For in the one Spirit we were all baptized into one body, Jews or Greeks, slaves or free, and we were all made to drink of one Spirit (1 Corinthians 12:13)," such the "there is no longer Jew or Greek, there is no longer slave or free, there is no longer male or female, for all... are one in Christ Jesus (Galatians 3:28)." Nonetheless, limpieza de sangre went viral and expanded. It traveled to the Americas with Christopher Columbus. It was integrated into protestant traditions through Martin Luther. Continental philosophers such as Voltaire and Kant introduced the idea into the academy, and Charles Darwin offered particularly appealing arguments that became the basis of scientific theories of human variation. Armed with a systematic ideology of race, European nations used the concept throughout the colonial period to explain their political domination over indigenous populations throughout the world.

In time, the global apportionment of legal rights along racial lines delineated hard social categories by which identification with certain earthly lineages, and a fear and rejection of stigmatized lineages, became at least as important, and in some case synonymous with, one's religious commitments. Even worse, because group identity often preempts personal identity, it becomes impossible for us as individuals to form meaningful bonds apart from or outside of the groups that define us. Nonetheless, we must earnestly seek deliverance.

Jesus Christ calls us to a single identity as one body in one Lord, one faith, and one baptism (Ephesians 4:4-6). The stakes are high because without a common identity, true unity is not possible. Without true unity, love fails. Without love, it is impossible to keep the new commandment that Christ has given to all believers (John 12:34).

It is our prayer that this book will help you to see the solidarity of humanity and the unity of all believers within the beautiful array of God's glorious creation. We hope that you will come to appreciate the richness of your heavenly family in a way that increases your joy and fellowship within the Body of Christ as you seek to follow Him.

Book Cover Design by Kevin Robert Keller - Kevin is a designer with an astute sense of maximizing beauty. Kevin launched his career on New York's Madison Avenue, creating advertising campaigns for Fortune 500 companies and two advertising agencies including Ogilvy. He has designed award-winning book covers and has applied his talents to an even wider range of design projects with great success. In book publishing, he has been a creative director (Regal) and senior art director (Multnomah). His sophistication with illustrations, photos, fonts and colors is masterful in drawing the human eye and heart. To connect with Kevin: <u>kevinrobertkeller-rdesign@gmail.com</u>. kevinrobertkeller.com.

Caricatures by Tony Smith – "Every successful event is built on the pillars of love and great entertainment." Tony Smith and his wife Kim are award-winning artists. They work with style and excellence and are in high demand.

See Dr. Alveda's collection of specially commissioned artwork at: <u>https://www.werenotcolorblindbook.com/</u>

MUSIC VIDEO
WE'RE NOT COLORBLIND

BY EVANGELIST ALVEDA KING

SCAN HERE TO LISTEN

NOTES

Chapter 1: A Meeting of the Hearts

Chapter 2: A Meeting of the Minds

1. This information was told to me by Clent Coker, who wrote the book *Barnsley Gardens at Woodlands*, my tour guide, and an article: Diane Wagner, "Magnolias of the Past: Julia and Julia of Barnsley Gardens" *Rome News Tribune*, April 12, 2011.

2. New Oxford American Dictionary

Chapter 3: Politics Aside

1. New Oxford American Dictionary

2. *My Life, My Love, My Legacy* by Coretta Scott King

Chapter 4: Different Sides of Town

1. *Hidden Figures*, directed by Theodore Melfi (Los Angeles, CA: Fox 2000 Pictures, 2016).

2. Ibid.

3. Ibid.

4. Kathryn Stockett, *The Help* (New York: G. P. Putnam's Sons, 2009).

Chapter 5: Shared Family Values

Chapter 6: Beloved Community Talks

1. Retrieved from: https://kinginstitute.stanford.edu/king-papers/documents/loving-your-enemies-sermon-delivered-dexter-avenue-baptist-church

Chapter 7: King Week 2018

1. James Russell Lowell, "Once to Every Man and Nation," 1845, https://hymnary.org/text/once_to_every_man_and_nation. Public domain.

Chapter 8: Colorblind? Why Not?

1. Williams, M. (2011, December 27). Colorblind Ideology is a Form of Racism. Retrieved from: https://www.psychologytoday.com/us/blog/culturally-speaking/201112/colorblind-ideology-is-form-racism

2. Benefiel, J. (2012). *Binding the strongman over America: Healing the land, transferring wealth, advancing the kingdom of God.* Benefiel Ministries, Inc.

Chapter 9: Living Together as Brothers and Sisters

1. Retrieved from: https://www.latimes.com/archives/la-xpm-1998-jan-19-me-10002-story.html

Chapter 10: One Blood, One Human Race

Chapter 11: Let the Light Shine

Chapter 12: Next Steps

ABOUT THE AUTHORS

Ginger Howard is a beloved motivator and spirited entrepreneur. As a graduate of the University of Georgia and owner of Ginger Howard Selections women's boutique, Ginger serves her constituency with boundless energy and a smile. The former co-host of Freedom Five, a popular radio talk show, she is also the founder of ATH Consulting Inc., a political consulting firm that helped elect Christian candidates to office. She is a gifted public speaker who loves to connect with her audience. Ginger is a two-term National Committeewoman for The Republican Party of Georgia and has been active in grassroots politics for the last two decades.

Alveda C. King is a creative Christian evangelist and civil rights activist and is also known for her creative contributions in film, music, politics, education and journalism. She is also a presidential appointee, spiritual advisor for the Trump National Diversity Coalition, an actress, singer, songwriter, blogger, author (including AMERICA RETURN TO GOD, KING TRUTHS, KING LEGACY COOKBOOK, KING RULES, WHO WE ARE IN CHRIST JESUS, LET FREEDOM RING, TENDER

MOMENTS ALONE WITH GOD), Fox News Contributor, and television and radio personality. As a former Georgia State Legislator, Director of Civil Rights for the Unborn for Priests for Life, and devoted mother and grandmother, she is also a guardian of the King Family Legacy. Alveda is the daughter of Reverend A. D. King and Mrs. Naomi King, the granddaughter of Reverend Martin Luther King, Sr. and Mrs. Alberta Williams King, and the niece of Dr. Martin Luther King, Jr.

Bishop Harry R. Jackson, the organizer of "The Reconciled Church" conference, is Senior Pastor of Hope Christian Church in the Washington, D.C., area. He is the founder and chairman of the High Impact Leadership Coalition, which works to protect the moral compass of America and be an agent of healing to our nation.

CPSIA information can be obtained
at www.ICGtesting.com
Printed in the USA
LVHW081012050321
680445LV00047B/342/J

9 781087 910246